A HISTORY OF
THE PERSE SCHOOL, CAMBRIDGE

PUBLISHERS.

CAMBRIDGE.

LONDON: MACMILLAN & CO., LIMITED
GLASGOW: MACLEHOSE, JACKSON & CO.

TOMB OF THE FOUNDER, DR. STEPHEN PERSE, IN THE CHAPEL OF
GONVILLE AND CAIUS COLLEGE, CAMBRIDGE

A HISTORY OF
THE PERSE SCHOOL
CAMBRIDGE

BY

J. M. GRAY, B.A.

KING'S COLLEGE, CAMBRIDGE

WITH SEVEN ILLUSTRATIONS

CAMBRIDGE
BOWES & BOWES
1921

COPYRIGHT

PUBLISHERS' NOTE

As the author has been unable, owing to absence from England, to see the book through the press, this work has been kindly undertaken by the Master of Jesus College and Mr. E. M. W. Tillyard, M.A., to whom our thanks are due.

We also wish to express our gratitude for the kind loan of pictures, from which the illustrations were taken, to the following: the Headmaster (Dr. W. H. D. Rouse), the Syndics of the Cambridge University Press, the Master and Fellows of Gonville and Caius College, the Proprietors of the *Illustrated London News*, R. Parker Smith, Esq., Mr. W. F. Turner, and Messrs. Rattee & Kett.

BOWES & BOWES.

August, 1921.

PREFACE

I wish to thank Dr. J. Venn, President of Gonville and Caius College, for giving me access to the college records and for imparting to me the valuable results of some of his own researches. I am indebted to the late Dr. Peile, Master of Christ's College, for useful information, both of his own and from the records of his college. My thanks are also due to the following for allowing me to look at college registers: Rev. T. A. Walker, LL.D. (Peterhouse); Mr. W. W. Rouse Ball, M.A. (Trinity); Mr. J. H. Sleeman, M.A. (Sidney, Sussex); the late Dr. S. A. Donaldson (Magdalene); Mr. D. L. Harris, M.A. (Downing).

I have made frequent use in the following pages of Cooper's *Memorials* and *Annals of Cambridge*.

J. M. GRAY.

CONTENTS

LIST OF ILLUSTRATIONS

CHAPTER I

STEPHEN PERSE

For a town of its size and importance, Cambridge was signally deficient in facilities for school education in the latter half of the sixteenth century. The population was recorded in 1587 as approximately five thousand, exclusive of members of the University. At the same date, Bury St. Edmunds and Ely each had less than half that number of inhabitants. Yet each of these places had a free grammar school, which was thrown open to the sons of the inhabitants. Two small schools were attached to King's and Trinity Colleges, but were confined exclusively to the choristers on those foundations; otherwise Cambridge possessed no endowed school.[1] The wants of the town were

[1] In 1443 Henry VI. established a school in connection with King's College. Provision was made therein for a master and sixteen choristers. In its origin it was a song school and was not in any way intended to provide for local requirements in education. It was by the Founder's directions confined exclusively to choristers, who were often recruited from places beyond Cambridge and its immediate neighbourhood. At the end of her reign Queen Mary

inadequately met by a few private schools kept
by members of the University.   These schools were
all short-lived.   None of them were conducted on
a scale sufficient to cope with the educational
requirements of the town.

Realising how backward Cambridge was in this
respect, the Corporation, in 1576, appointed nine
of their number as a committee " to devise and put
in wrytinge some good devise for the erecting of a
grammer schoole within the said towne, and how
ye charges of the same maie be borne and raysed."
Later in the same year, a further committee of
eleven was appointed to " rate and assesse what
somes every person shall paie towards ye charges
thereof."   Apparently the difficulties attendant
on the levying of such a rate put an end to the
discussion, for nothing further was heard of the
proposal.

As public enterprise had failed, the inhabitants
of Cambridge were obliged to wait until a private
benefactor should provide for their needs.   The
first step towards the endowment of a school was
made by William Bridon, who had entered Clare

made provision for a similar school at Trinity, which was to comprise
a master and ten choristers.   This also was primarily a song school.
In 1570 the teaching of grammar in Cambridge University was
prohibited by statute, except in the case of the choristers of these
colleges.

Hall in the same year as the Corporation had put forward their proposal. Bridon was apparently a man of considerable means. After taking his degree, he married and settled in Cambridge. He died in or about 1590, and by his will bequeathed the sum of one hundred marks for the founding of a grammar school, or for some other work for the encouragement of learning.

Unfortunately Bridon's gift was destined to lie useless for a quarter of a century. His bequest was deemed quite insufficient for the erection and endowment of a grammar school even when it was supplemented by another sum of one hundred marks. This second gift came from Thomas Cropley, who was also a member of Clare Hall, where he entered as a sizar in June, 1577. Cropley was evidently an intimate friend of Bridon, for in his will Bridon gives a legacy to one of Cropley's daughters. By his marriage with Anne, sister of Clement Hodson, alderman of Cambridge, Cropley was brought into contact with many of the leading townspeople. From them he came to realise what were the educational deficiencies of Cambridge. By his will (dated November 24th, 1607), he added another hundred marks to Bridon's, hoping that the work so long delayed might at last be carried out. Nevertheless his hope was not immediately realised.

The money lay idle for eight years, for two hundred marks was considered no more adequate for the purpose than one hundred.

Another graduate of the University, who took an interest in local affairs, was Stephen Perse, fellow of Caius College. He was senior to both Bridon and Cropley, for he had entered Caius in 1564. From the fact that he assumed the arms of the family it is to be presumed that he was connected with the Perses of Northwold, Norfolk. Of this family, the earliest known is a John Perse, who died in 1505, leaving considerable bequests to Northwold. It was his son (also John) who, in 1560, received the grant of arms, which have since become associated with the Perse School.[1] Stephen's father was also John, and was in all probability a grandson of the first John. This third John was originally of Great Massingham in Norfolk, but subsequently removed to Swaffham Market in the same county. Stephen Perse was born at Great Massingham in or about 1548. According to the Caius admission register Stephen's father was " mediocris fortunae," that is to say probably of the rank of a superior yeoman farmer. He had one other son. He was

[1] Sable, a chevron ermine, between three cockatrice's heads erased argent, lingued gules : and Crest, on a torse argent and sable, a pelican or vulning herself proper. Motto : *Qui facit per alium facit per se.*

sufficiently wealthy to put his boys to school at Norwich, and to send Stephen to Cambridge as a pensioner.

Of the undergraduate days of Stephen Perse we know nothing. He took his B.A. degree in 1569. His name appears last on the *Ordo* for that year, but as this list can in no way be said to be a true order of merit, and as two years later Perse was elected to a fellowship at his college, there is no reason for believing that his academic attainments were mediocre. Two examples of his classical work survive. One appears in a collection of Latin verses published by the University in 1603, in commemoration of the accession of James I. The contribution made by Perse is an ode of welcome to the new king. Like most of the other pieces in the collection, it is faultless both in its Latinity and its versification : otherwise the verses possess no remarkable merit, and are inclined to be bombastic. The other set of verses penned by Perse are to be found on the monument erected to his memory in Caius College Chapel.[1] The most that can be said of these pieces is that they are typical of the period, being neither below nor above the average. The

[1] Cp. p. 21. A set of verses, which bear a strong resemblance to the other known works of Perse, appears on the mural monument erected in St. Edward's Church, Cambridge, to the memory of his brother-in-law, William Becke.

" six mapps," mentioned in an inventory of his goods which was compiled after his death, perhaps indicate a taste for geography. But Perse was clearly not a bookish man, for the same document informs us that his library was appraised at less than one half the value of his wearing apparel.

At this period most of the fellowships at Caius College were allotted to the study of Theology or Law, but Dr. Caius had recently added to the foundation two fellowships attached to the study of Medicine. On his election, Stephen Perse " sett downe his profession in divinity." On May 7th, 1573, he was ordained both priest and deacon by the Bishop of Peterborough, but does not appear to have ever held any ecclesiastical preferment. Shortly after his ordination, he " was permitted and furthered " by Dr. Legge, then Master of Caius, " to chaunge both his sayd profession and his place to another fellowshipp, whereby he professed physick." Within a very short period he again returned to the study of divinity. Finally, in 1581, he took the degree of Doctor of Medicine and was permitted by Legge " to professe physick in the same place which he last desired, and by consent was graunted, for a divine." [1]

---

[1] Heywood and Wright, *Cambridge University Transactions during the Puritan Controversies,* i. 325, 330.

All these changes had been sanctioned by the Master of the College but not by the Fellows, who complained that the last transaction was " to ther mislikinge." The Fellows were at variance with Legge in other matters. In 1581 they petitioned the Chancellor of the University concerning their grievances. The preferential treatment accorded to Perse forms one of their charges against the Master, but nothing further is heard of this particular complaint. Perse was allowed to retain his fellowship, and to devote himself to the study of medicine. The animosity against him died out, and in time he came to be on the best of terms with the other Fellows of his college. He proved himself a competent man of affairs, and from 1579 to 1593 acted as college bursar. In 1589 he was chosen to represent the faculty of medicine on the Caput—the executive council of the University.

The interests of Stephen Perse were not confined to Caius College. After 1581, he came in contact with people outside the University. Prior to that date he had, in accordance with the usual custom, taken pupils. After obtaining his degree in medicine he abandoned the greater part of his tutorial work and practised as a physician in the town. For this new sphere he had an able rival in William Butler of Clare Hall, the physician of

James I. and friend of Nicholas Ferrar. Butler was perhaps the most renowned English physician of his age, but " he was a man of great moodes." Some of his cures were effected in an alarming manner, and the uncertainty of his temper must have deterred many a patient from resorting to him.[1] Conventional methods would be more popular than the extraordinary treatment which people were liable to suffer at Butler's hands. Patients would, therefore, prefer Perse to his more brilliant contemporary, who " would suffer persons of quality to wayte sometimes some houres at his dore, with coaches, before he would receive them." There was, however, no professional jealousy between the two, for Perse made a bequest to Butler " to make him a ringe in token of my especiall love to him." Perse was also on good terms with another local physician, Isaac Barrow. Perhaps Perse succeeded to Barrow's practice, for James, " sometymes servant to Dor Barroe," subsequently entered the service of the former as surgeon. Perse was godfather to Barrow's son, Isaac, the future Bishop of St. Asaph.

Late in life Stephen Perse married. No definite date can be assigned for this marriage and the christian name of the lady is not known. She was

---

[1] In Cooper, *Annals of Cambridge*, iii. 119-124, will be found some account of Butler's eccentricities.

the daughter of Simon Ellvin, of Heveningham Park, near Norwich, attorney-at-law. Her mother, her sister Eleanor, and her brother Thomas, who was about thirteen years of age when his brother-in-law deceased, are all mentioned in Stephen's will. As Perse makes no mention of his wife in his will, it must be concluded that she died before 1615. His mother-in-law is mentioned there in terms of the deepest possible affection. Stephen's memories of his married days must therefore have been happy.

Although in his latter days he was left a widower and childless, Stephen Perse was not without kinsfolk in the town of Cambridge. Mrs. Ellvin resided with her son Thomas in St. Edward's parish. At Trinity there was another Stephen Perse, who became a divine and fellow of his college. Yet another kinsman was Martin Perse, the head of the Northwold branch of the family, who came to reside in Cambridge in the early years of the seventeenth century, and concerning whom this book will have more to say. On the death of his brother, John of Swaffham Market, Dr. Perse became the guardian of his niece Katherine,[1] who also settled in Cambridge. In 1604 Katherine Perse married William Becke, a barrister of the Middle Temple, who had formerly been her uncle's pupil at Caius.

[1] *Ely Episcopal Records*, p. 254.

The Beckes resided in Luthburne Lane in the refectory of the Augustinian Friars. In 1615 they had a family of four sons and several daughters.

Thirty years of practice as a physician enabled Stephen Perse to amass a considerable fortune—" ultra communem Academicorum sortem," as the writer of the *Annals* of Caius College somewhat enviously comments. With his savings he purchased the old refectory and close of the Augustinian Friars at Cambridge, where his brother-in-law resided. He was the owner of other property in Cambridge, as well as freehold and copyhold lands at Impington and Cottenham in the county.

But wealth was not all that his doctoring brought him. He found himself brought closely into touch with the townspeople of Cambridge. In the earlier days his college pupils had been friends or the sons of friends from Norfolk, and persons of some affluence : in his later days they were without exception boys of quite humble origin. Many of them were local boys. In some cases he gave them instruction to prepare them for the University. Bartholomew Church, for instance, was grounded by him in the principles of rhetoric and dialectics, before he was admitted at Caius in 1601. The relations between the tutor and his pupils were often very homely. Three of the very last of his pupils

obtained special mention in his will. The kindliness, moreover, was not confined entirely to these
boys. Perse struck up friendships with many of
his neighbours in Cambridge, the great majority
being people of a very humble class. " James my
surgeon," " Henry Prist my barber," and Perse's
two menservants are all remembered in their master's
will. Other friends, whom Perse was careful not to
forget, were evidently patients or people with whom
his practice brought him in contact. He was
obviously something more than a physician to many
Cambridge families, and after his death his kindliness
must have been greatly missed in many homes. He
did something more than distribute promiscuous
doles to obtain a reputation for charity. He learnt
to study, and by studying to understand, what were
the real and lasting wants of the town. Having no
family dependent on him, he was in a position to
evolve a scheme devoting a considerable portion of
his wealth to the fulfilment of those wants.

Perse's will is dated September 27th, 1615—
only three days before his death, but from its
elaborateness and the minuteness of its details it is
quite clear that it was not a disposition of his estate
hurriedly conceived upon his death-bed It was a
scheme over which much time and thought had been
expended. He had two objects in view when he

formulated his plans. In the first place, like so many Elizabethans, he took a great interest in the social problems of the day and had the desire for their solution close at heart. In the second place, he watched with dismay the dissensions between the Town and University, and hoped by the creation of a common interest to pave the way for reconciliation. First of all, as a patriotic son, he made a special bequest to the poor of his birthplace and the neighbouring parish of Harpley. Then he proceeded to map out his plan for the benefit of the Town and University. The central feature of the whole scheme was a free grammar school, and this was to be the connecting link between the two corporations. Perse did not, however, confine his plan solely to the erection of a school. One of his chief objects was to prevent—or at any rate to relieve—destitution as much as possible. Prevention could be effected primarily by training up children to habits of industry : hence a *raison d'être* for the school. Poverty could be further mitigated by providing for the aged, who had merited peace and security after a life of industry. Perse, therefore, proposed to erect an almshouse adjoining his school for six poor widows, preference being given to parishioners of St. Michael's and St. Edward's.

The school, however, was to be something more than a piece of machinery in a general scheme of social reform. Perse hoped that its foundation might ultimately put an end to the bitter rivalry between Town and University, which he had witnessed throughout his life. It is unnecessary to go into details of the many conflicts between the two. Suffice it to say that in 1615, the very year in which Perse died, the quarrel became acute, when the Town petitioned the Crown for a new Charter conferring an extension of their privileges and the University presented a counter petition alleging that the proposed extension would be an encroachment on their own rights. The bequest of Stephen Perse is in significant contrast to the bitter feeling displayed at the time by both parties. He was anxious to prepare the way for reconciliation at once, for one of his very first requests is that the three University esquire bedels will co-operate with his old friend, Isaac Barrow, and three aldermen of the town, mentioned by name, in order to carry out his scheme. He devises a certain portion of his property to the seven upon trust, to sell the same and expend the proceeds in carrying out the trusts of his will.

Perse hoped to heal the breach by making the school essentially a Town school, and yet giving it a very direct connection with the University. With that object in view, he imitated the twin foundations set up by William of Wykeham and Henry VI.   He did not need to create a college, for one was already at hand.   At his own college of Caius he founded six scholarships and six fellowships, for election to which special preference was to be given to boys educated at his school.   The scholars were each to receive £4 *per annum* and the fellows £6.   They were all to be housed in a special building which Perse directed to be built at a cost to his estate of £500.

Perse, furthermore, described in some detail the principles that were to regulate his school.   The first governors were to be his three executors. These were Valentine Carey (then Master of Christ's and Dean of St. Paul's, afterwards Bishop of Exeter); his kinsman, Martin Perse; and the Founder's solicitor, Robert Spicer, to whom Perse left a ring of the value of £3 " for ould remembrance of friendshippe."   These three were to frame rules for the conduct of the school, which they were to submit to the Justices of Assize for revision or confirmation.   The appointment of the masters and of the Perse scholars and fellows of Caius was to be in their hands.   After the decease of the last survivor of these three, the management of the school was to be entrusted to the master and four senior fellows of Caius. As remuneration for their services as governors the fellows were each to receive an annual stipend of thirty shillings : the Master was to be paid three pounds. The school itself was to be erected on " all those garden grounds parcell of the Fryars,[1] now in the occupacion of John Paske, William Smithson, and Benjamin Prime, or either of them, and also all that parcell of ground lying between the said gardens and the wallnut trees in Fryars close, and . . . . . the garden grounds and tenements now Mr. Ward's, adjoyning upon the said gardens,"—that is to say at the south end of the street which was then known as Luthburne Lane, leading from the present Benet Street to Pembroke Street. The almshouses already mentioned were to be built within the circuit of the same grounds.

On this site the executors were to erect " a convenient house to be used for a Grammar Free Schoole, with one lodging chamber for the Master and another for the Usher." These two were to be graduates of Cambridge University. The Master was to be of the degree of Master of Arts at least, and to receive a stipend of forty pounds a year. The Usher was to have a salary of twenty pounds, and was expected to be a Bachelor of Arts at least.

---

[1] *Sc.* the Augustinian friars.

The two were to teach gratuitously five score scholars born in Cambridge, Barnwell, Chesterton, or Trumpington, "and no more, nor any other." This last injunction should be noted : this provision was intended to prevent the school from being swamped with non-foundationers to the detriment of the foundationers—that is to say, to emphasise the fact that the school was primarily intended for the benefit of the Town. Any boy who had attended the school for at least three years was to be eligible for a Perse scholarship, and in the due course of events a Perse fellowship, at Caius. Furthermore, preference was to be given to boys formerly educated at the school in appointment to any vacancy in the posts of master or usher.

All the foregoing regulations reveal the thoroughness with which the Founder planned his scheme in his desire to avoid all ambiguity in the interpretation of his will.   In face of this it is somewhat surprising to find how very unsatisfactory is his treatment of the financial side of the scheme.   Perse instructed his executors to sell his property in St. Sepulchre's parish, known as the Horn, to provide the necessary capital for erecting the school buildings.   The executors are also "to use their best means for obtaining of the two hundred marks heretofore devised by Mr. Thomas Cropley and Bridon " for furthering the same object. Perse desired to guarantee a permanent and non-fluctuating income to his charity. With this object in view he proposed to offer upon receipt of satisfactory security a sum of £2000 to the corporation of Norwich, and a sum of £1000 to each of the corporations of Cambridge, Bury, and Lynn. These sums were to be regarded as loans, and the recipients were to pay interest at the rate of five per cent. annually into the funds of the trust. The corporations were not to be allowed to exercise their own discretion as to the investment of the money thus lent. Perse gave specific instructions as to the manner in which they were to obtain the required interest. The capital was to be lent out upon good security in sums not exceeding forty pounds to young tradesmen belonging to the four different towns at five per cent. interest and no more. The Founder thus calculated that the five thousand pounds capital would produce an income of £250, which would be sufficient to meet the expenses of the trust.

If the Norwich and the other three corporations accepted these terms, there was a perpetual guaranteed income for Perse's trust. But would the four think the terms worth accepting? Would they consent to become revenue collectors to the Perse trustees? The Founder was short-sighted in that he did not see that the answer to these questions would most obviously be a decided negative. The bargain was a very one-sided one. The sole benefit the towns could hope to derive was the possibility of indirect improvement of trade by the encouragement of struggling beginners. Against this were to be set hard facts. The corporations were to receive no remuneration whatever for their services as collectors, and they were asked to meet all deficiencies out of their own pockets. As they were precluded from exacting anything more than five per cent.—at that time half the recognised legal rate of interest—they were asked to run very considerable risks. The bargain was not good enough, and accordingly each corporation renounced its legacy, when the terms of the will were made known.

Apparently Perse in his lifetime received an intimation that his legacies might not be deemed altogether acceptable and he prepared for such a contingency. It is this alternative scheme which shows the most want of care. Perse added the following clause to his will :—

" Provided alwayes and my minde is, that if any inconvenience be by my Executours and supervisours seen into that the saide ccl^{li} per annum shall not be sufficiently assured, to continue in perpetuity by such assurances as may be taken from the said Corporations (which I desire may be for the good of many of the said corporations), then I will that the said D^{li} so bequeathed as aforesaid to the said Corporations of Norwich, Cambridge, Burie, and Lin, or so much thereof as shall not be secured, be by my Executours . . . . bestowed and layde out in the purchase of lands to raise or make up the revenue of CCL^{li} per annum ultra reprisas . . . . Soe alwayes as the yearly revenue thereof be yearely from time to time received, layd out, and paid, in such manner, to such uses, intents, and purposes, and to such persons as before in this my will is appointed to be paid in perpetuity."

At first sight this insertion appears quite satisfactory, but in considering Perse's will it must be borne in mind that the testator always clung to the idea that the income of the trust would be a fixed one. Even when he sanctioned the investment of the capital in land, he still thought that the land would bring in a steady rental of £250—no less and no more. Not only did he consider that the income would be permanent; he also carefully specified the precise amount which was to be paid to each individual object of his benefaction. In all these payments amount to £243 14s. 8d., leaving a surplus of £6 5s. 4d. Perse thought that this surplus was always going to be six odd pounds, and no more. Accordingly, without the slightest possible hesitation, he directed that it should be "from time to time bestowed upon such charitable uses, as my Executours for their times, and after my supervisours, shall think fit." So long as this residue did not exceed six or seven pounds, this discretionary power was a matter of no great importance; but when this surplus began to increase—indeed eventually to exceed the amount ear-marked for the special objects of the will—it became an instrument with which unconscientious trustees might stultify the intentions of the testator. As will be seen on a later page, it was quite possible for an unscrupulous set of trustees to regard themselves as the deserving objects of Stephen Perse's charity and to leave the principal objects of his will to subsist on their bare statutable payments—payments which were rendered all the more meagre by the decrease in their relative value as years went on. It was not until 1837 that this loophole for legal malversation was closed by order of a court of law. During the intervening two centuries the school was to suffer severely for the want of foresight with which the Founder expressed his wishes.

It would, however, be unjust as well as ungrateful to blame the Founder for being unable to foresee the future. The clause empowering the trustees to invest in land is a hasty insertion made in all probability as Perse lay on his death-bed. For the moment the intimation, that the corporations might renounce their legacies, looked as if it might bring the great scheme to an untimely end. But Perse was not the man to be easily frustrated. He endeavoured to adapt his plans to changed circumstances, but his alterations were hurriedly made and necessarily suffered from the imperfections of haste.

The will bears date September 27th, 1615. Three days later Stephen Perse passed away. He was buried in Caius College Chapel, where a large mural monument was erected to his memory by his relations. He is there represented in effigy kneeling in his doctor's robes. Above him are his crest and coat of arms, now familiar as the armorial bearings of the school. Below are the following lines composed by Perse himself :—

Praenomen Stephanus, cognomen Perse vocatum,
  Sola Deo soli vita corona fuit.
Cum vivente Deo remanet mihi vita perennis,
  Jamque cano soli παντότε δόξα θεῷ.
Haec moriens cecini lecturo Perseus ipse :
  Non ulli melius quam mihi notus eram.

Christin, surnamed, Stephen Perse I hight,
  Sole life with God alone, my crowne my light,
    With living God eternall life I live.
    This now my song : to sole God praise I give,
This Epitaph by me Perse was devized,
To none else my thoughts better were comprised.

In the town of Cambridge was destined to rise a greater monument still—a monument which fittingly commemorates a life which, though quiet and uneventful, was well and nobly spent.

CHAPTER II

THE EARLY DAYS OF THE PERSE. (1618-36)

Two of Perse's executors, Carey and Spicer, very soon relieved themselves of their duties. By an indenture dated November 17, 1615, they confided the sole execution of the will to the third executor, Martin Perse. Such an arrangement was not unnatural. Although residence was expected of him as Master of Christ's, Carey was frequently absent from Cambridge. As Bishop of Exeter and Dean of St. Paul's he had a good many other irons in the fire. Spicer was advanced in years. He acted as Registrary to the Perse trust to the day of his death, but the prospect of setting the Founder's scheme in good order could not have been inviting to a man of his age. Accordingly the sole responsibility devolved upon Martin Perse, who, from his intimate association with Stephen during his latter days, was eminently fitted to carry out the trust according to the spirit as well as the letter of the will.

The Founder's fear that the corporations would not accept the proffered loans proved by no means unfounded. All four renounced their legacies, and the executor had to look about for land in which to invest the trust capital. In 1617 he purchased the manor of Frating and other adjoining properties in Essex. Next year he conveyed this purchase to the then master and four senior fellows of Caius upon the trusts of the will. Apparently not all the available capital was invested in this estate, and the rental fell short of the required two hundred and fifty pounds by £22 1s. 0d. For several years the residue remained uninvested and the deficiency in income was made up by an annual payment from Martin Perse. In 1627 the transaction was placed upon a permanent and more satisfactory basis. In consideration of the grant to him of liberty to cut the woods and underwoods of Frating, Perse conveyed to Caius seventy-seven acres of arable land at Bassingbourne in Cambridgeshire.

By the beginning of 1617, Martin Perse found himself in a position to take steps for the erection of the grammar school and almshouses. All outstanding leases had been bought in, and the property rounded off by the purchase of the adjoining land. The Horn was sold, but it is not clear whether the two hundred marks bequeathed by Bridon and

Cropley were obtained. A sufficient sum of money was, however, forthcoming for building purposes. The foundations were laid in February, 1617.[1] By Michaelmas, 1618, the building was ready for the reception of masters and boys. It lay at the south end of what was then known as Luthburne Lane, but subsequently changed its title to Free School Lane. To the south of it and facing the King's Ditch lay the " six severall low tenements " built for the almswomen. At the north end of the Friars' Close and just opposite St. Benet's Church there still stood the old refectory of the Augustinian Friars. The Founder had bequeathed this house to his niece, Katherine Becke, whose husband had died in 1614. Shortly after Stephen's death she married Martin Perse, and the two resided in the house until 1632, watching the little seedling planted by their kinsman pass safely through the critical stages of these early days. Long after the house had passed into other hands its former connection with the family of the Founder's sister was perpetuated by the familiar Perse coat of arms carved " over ye chimney-piece on ye wainscot " of the dining room and the arms of the Becke family in the " matted room." [2]

[1] Bowtell MS. vii. p. 2722.
[2] *Warren's Book* (ed. A. W. W. Dale), pp. 123, 140.

OLD SCHOOL IN FREE SCHOOL LANE (EXTERIOR), CIRCA 1840

As the school buildings did not entirely cover the remainder of the site, there was an open space left on the north side. This was made into a garden which, in 1621, was let on a fifty years' lease at an annual rent of forty shillings, the said rent to be expended on all necessary repairs to the school. The school itself stood between this garden and the almshouses. It consisted of three sides of a quadrangle facing the lane. In the centre was the schoolroom. Flanking it on either side were the houses of the Master and Usher. The entrance from the lane to this quadrangle was through a gateway surmounted by the arms of Stephen Perse. Within the gateway was a small court some twenty yards square. Entrance to the schoolroom was obtained by two narrow passages passing through the houses of the respective masters. The room itself was sixty-four feet in length, twenty feet in width, and in height up to the cornices some sixteen feet. The whole was surmounted by a fine open roof. The room was lighted by mullioned windows filled with panes of thick diamond-shaped glass. Except for the roof, there was no attempt at decoration.

The early Masters inhabited the house on the north side of the school, but at some period during the eighteenth century they changed their residence for that of the Usher.   From an inventory of the fittings of the Master's house made in 1687 we can obtain some idea of what the interior was like.   It had an upper floor as well as garrets just under the roof.   Entrance was obtained by a door leading from the forecourt straight into the parlour. Directly opposite to this door was another leading out into the garden behind.   Above this parlour was the study.   The kitchen, " butteries," and pantry were all crowded on the ground floor.   Outside was a considerable garden flanking the school on the north and west sides.   In it the Master had a summer house and—more important still from the domestic point of view—a well and pump.

The Usher's house was probably more or less a replica of that of the Master.   Apparently it was not so large, for in 1664 the Usher paid tax for only two chimneys as against the Master's four.   The Usher was not so fortunate as to possess a garden, unless he shared that of the Master.

Such then were the buildings which were to be the home of the Perse for nearly two centuries.   At Michaelmas, 1618, the Master and Usher were appointed and the first boys admitted.   It was not until 1624 that the Perse Account Books begin to record the names of the two Masters.   Thomas Lovering is the first Master mentioned in these books, but from various college admission registers we learn that he was appointed four or five years before 1624. He was obviously the man for the executors of Stephen Perse to appoint. About 1614, Thomas Ellvin, the Founder's young brother-in-law, went to a school kept by the future Master of the Perse in St. Edward's Church. Stephen Perse must, therefore, have known and appreciated Lovering's undoubted teaching ability. Graduating from Pembroke Hall in 1615, Lovering was not long afterwards appointed headmaster of the King's College School, where he continued until his appointment to the Perse. Some of his verses—both English and Latin—are still extant,[1] and exhibit a literary facility of a high level. Both as a teacher and pioneer he was well fitted to do the spade work required in a new school. No appointment could have been more gratifying to Stephen Perse had he been alive.

No permanent rules for the conduct of the school were made until 1622. Then both Carey and Spicer joined with Martin Perse to frame ordinances, which in compliance with Founder's directions were

[1] These are to be found in the following works : Ralph Winterton's *Aphorismes of Hippocrates* (1633), William Hawkins' *Corolla Varia* (1634), *Lacrymae Cantabrigienses* (1619), *Cant. Dolor et Solamen* (1625), and *Epithalamium . . . Principum Caroli Regis et H. Mariae* (1625).

duly submitted to the two Justices of Assize for confirmation. From these rules much can be gleaned about the life of the early members of the Perse School. As the Founder had requested, free scholars' places were limited to one hundred boys from Cambridge, Barnwell, Chesterton, and Trumpington. The executors did not, however, in further conformity with the instructions laid down in the will restrict the advantages of the school to free scholars only. Nevertheless, whilst throwing the Perse open to non-free scholars, they carefully took steps to prevent the headmaster from neglecting the free scholars for those who paid. They strictly forbad him to take in other than foundationers " except the Master and Usher doe take to them such further sufficient help as the Executors think fit."

The manner of admitting a free scholar seems remarkably simple to those who live in an age of competitive examinations. The candidate's parents applied to the churchwarden of his native parish for a written statement that the boy was born or baptised in Cambridge or one of the three privileged villages.[1] The father or mother brought this certificate to the executors (and after their deaths to the Master and

---

[1] Some sixty or seventy of these birth and baptismal certificates can still be seen in the Caius College Treasury.

four senior fellows of Caius).   If there was only one
candidate in the field, the governors of the school
would admit the boy at once on receipt of such a
certificate.   In the event of two or more applicants
for a single vacancy, it was directed that " a poor
man's child shall be preferred to it before a rich, so
that he makes suit for it in time."   The parent of
the successful candidate received from the governors
a written order of admission, which he presented to
the headmaster.   Apparently the headmaster used
sometimes to anticipate this order and receive the
boy a week or a fortnight before the admission was
formally granted.[1]   Upon entrance all new boys
were required to pay twelvepence to the Usher " in
lieu of his pains for writing their names into the
book and tables."

These formalities once finished, the boy settled
down to the routine of school life.   He was an early
riser, for he was expected to be in his place at the
school by six o'clock in the morning.   At half-past
six the scholars assembled for prayers, after which

[1] Such appears to have been the case under a later Master, as can
be gathered from the following extracts from Alderman Samuel
Newton's diary for the year 1666-7 : " Feb: 12th. On Tewsday was
the first time John Newton my sonne went to the Grammar Free
Schoole in Cambridge—Feb:26: Joh. Newton was entred by Dr
Bradyes order into the Free Schoole.   On Tewsday D^{or} Robt
Brady Ma^{r} of Caijus Coll: gaue mee his order under his hand to
Mr Griffith ma^{r} of the said schoole for his receiving the said John
Newton in the same schoole."

ordinary lessons continued until eleven. The afternoon's work began at one and lasted until five, when
the boys again came together for prayers before
dispersing to their homes.

The curriculum provided for teaching " as well
in good manners as in all other instruction and
learning fit to be learned in a Grammar School."
This general instruction would give the Master
scope to employ what methods of teaching he liked.
Latin would be the chief scholastic exercise, the
thorough teaching of the Roman tongue being, as
the name implies, the very purpose for which
grammar schools were designed. On his arrival at
the Perse, a boy would, therefore, be expected to be
equipped with some knowledge of the rudiments
acquired either at home or at a petty school. For
instance, John Newton, who was admitted to the
school in 1667, shortly before his eighth birthday,
was able soon after his admission to write in his
father's diary in a sprawling hand with the guidance
of lines ruled in pencil. At the Perse almost the
whole of the schoolboy's time would be devoted to
the study of Latin. In his first year he would be
fully occupied in learning the elements of Latin
accidence, and would probably be expected to
commit to memory lists of common words. In his
second year, after fully mastering grammar, he

would turn to an elementary phrase-book such as *Sententiae Pueriles,* thereby becoming familiar with the structure and idioms of the language.   In his third year conversational methods of teaching would be introduced, and one of the many manuals bearing the title of *Confabulationes Pueriles* would be placed in his hands.   The boys in the higher forms would read Ovid, " Tully," and Virgil, and in the highest form of all would gain an insight into Latin drama. Seneca would be the most popular tragedian, and the plays of Terence and Plautus would also be read and perhaps acted.   Greek would probably not be learnt until a boy had reached one of the higher forms. Boys at the top of the school might possibly begin to learn Hebrew.   A boy who remained at the Perse for some five or six years would have a good colloquial knowledge of Latin.   Towards the end of his school career the constant speaking of the language would be indispensable and the writing of Latin letters would be insisted upon.   As the history of the Perse will show, the small Latin and less Greek taught in the ordinary seventeenth century grammar school awakened the latent powers of more than one schoolboy of humble origin and served a useful purpose in mental discipline.

Little or no provision was made for other subjects which are now regarded as indispensable in secondary education. We hear nothing of the teaching of mathematics. Dead languages had priority over all other branches of learning. John Newton had to wait till his school days were over before he could learn " the French language " and the gentle art of playing on the " Base Viall."

As a rule boys left at an earlier age than is usual nowadays. Those who did not intend to proceed to the University were generally apprenticed to some local tradesmen between the ages of twelve and fifteen. Other boys went up to college when they were between fourteen and seventeen years old. During the eighteen years of his headmastership, Lovering sent a large number of boys to the University—probably a far larger number than came at that time from any other school of the same size. About one hundred of his former pupils can be traced as having entered different colleges at Cambridge, and of these fifteen became fellows of colleges. A certain number of these were attracted to Caius College by the prospect of obtaining a Perse scholarship and fellowship, but a large number entered at other colleges as pensioners, or, in the case of poorer boys, as sizars, who sometimes paid their college bills " in wares " in default of money.[1]

---

[1] An example of a former Perse boy paying his bill partly " in wares " is given in Peile's *Biographical Register of Christ's College,*

A Perse boy, who had graduated at the University, had a special preference in selection for any vacancy in the post of Master or Usher. If we take into consideration the salaries usually paid to members of the teaching profession in the seventeenth century, both these posts were well paid. The Master received the forty pounds' stipend directed to be paid to him by the Founder. In further conformity with the will of Stephen Perse he was required to be of the standing of Master of Arts at least. The executors further ordained that he was not to hold any fellowship or ecclesiastical preferment in conjunction with his mastership under penalty of forfeiture of his post at the school. The ordinances did not require the Master to be in his place at the school before seven o'clock in the morning. They also allowed him to be absent during school time for not more than one hour during the day.

The Usher was not permitted so much liberty as the Master. He had to be in attendance during the whole of school hours. His stipend was twenty pounds per annum, and he was required to be a Bachelor of Arts at least. Like the Master, he was not allowed to hold preferment outside the school.

vol. i. p. 383.   The first payment received from the father of Jeremy Goose, the boy in question, is " taken at his shop from his admission 26 April 1627 to 16 August 1628—2^{li} 8s 4d."   The final bill is partly paid " in wares."

The Usher was also expected to undertake the duties
of registrar. He was required to keep an admission
book recording the names of all free scholars as they
entered the school with the date and year of their
election. As has been noticed already, he received
twelvepence from each new scholar by way of
remuneration. It was further directed that the
Usher should " from time to time bring the said
book to the Executours during their lives, and after
to the Supervisours, that the schollers so elected
may also be written in the book remaining with
the Executours or Supervisours, that they may
both agree." This duplication was not enough
for the executors. Their sixth ordinance decreed
that there shall be a small handsome frame of board,
with a paper pasted thereon, " wherein all the free
schollers names shall be from time to time written
by the usher of the school, and as any of the schollers
goes away, his name shall be crossed out, and the
schollers name put in that is new chosen, and
the time of his election. And once every year the
table shall be renewed by taking off the old paper
and putting on a new with all the free schollers
names, written thereupon that then are remaining
in their places, which Table shall continually hang
up in the school, to that end that every one that
cometh into the school may see whether the full

number of free schollers be there from time to time taught according to Dr. Perse's Will."

Had all these records been preserved the historian of the Perse would have had a plenteous store from which to gather materials for his work. Unfortunately, the ushers little knew how precious were the documents entrusted to their care. Not a single complete register survives. Two loose pages from one book [1] are all that remain of what might have been an invaluable store of historical matter.

There is no record in the Perse Accounts of any payment being made to any assistant master except the Usher. At one period, however, Lovering had a "further sufficient help," as enjoined by the school ordinances, to assist in the teaching of non-foundationers. Presumably the Master paid this assistant out of his own pocket. The assistant in question was a Mr. Burgis, who, about 1630, was appointed Master of Saffron Walden Grammar School. He was destined to regret his promotion, for divers inhabitants of Walden " brought him to such infinite suits and charges, that, being now in holy orders, he is likely to be turned out into the wide world a-begging." [2]

[1] Now to be seen in the Caius College Treasury.

[2] *Calendar of State Papers (Domestic),* ccxlvi. (letter dated Feb. 8. 1636-7) and ccxlvii. (letter dated Feb. 1637). Mr. Burgis is apparently to be identified with Peter Burgess, of St. John's College,

Burgis went to Saffron Walden at the general request of the townspeople—a fact which testifies to the reputation enjoyed by Perse masters at this time. The fame of the school reached further than neighbouring counties. We find among Lovering's pupils boys from such distant places as Northumberland and County Cork. Parents of exalted rank also entrusted their sons to Lovering's care. Talbot Pepys of Impington, Recorder of Cambridge, sent two of his sons to the school. [1]   Sir William Beecher, Clerk to the Privy Council of James I., withdrew his son from Eton to place him under Lovering,[2] and Lord Chaworth of Ardagh sent his second son to the school. As the school ordinances directed, the free scholars were most frequently drawn from the humbler walks in life. With all its deficiencies the seventeenth century grammar school was democratic—a quality regrettably absent in many of its modern successors.

Lovering was fortunate in having the ready co-

Cambridge (M.A. 1630), who was ordained deacon (Peterborough) September 20, 1629, and licensed to practise medicine in 1634.

[1] Talbot was great-uncle of Samuel Pepys, the diarist. Roger and John Pepys, the two sons here referred to, are frequently mentioned in their cousin's diary. Roger Pepys was Recorder and Member of Parliament for Cambridge 1661-79. John Pepys was Fellow of Trinity Hall in 1641.

[2] The son, William Beecher, was Fellow of St. John's, Cambridge, 1631-47.

operation of those whom the founder had requested to carry out his will. Alderman Robert Lukin, one of the seven devisees for the sale of the Founder's property, sent his son James to the school. Still closer was the connection between the school and the near relations of the Founder, more especially Martin Perse. Two step-sons of Martin Perse, Perse Becke and William Becke, were among the first boys to be admitted to the school. Both of them proceeded to Caius, where they became Fellows on their great-uncle's foundation. At a later date Martin Perse sent his own sons, Valentine and Martin, to the school. They subsequently became scholars on the Perse foundation at Caius.[1]

Martin Perse, the elder, did not allow his interest in the school to flag after he had finished the task of establishing it and setting the machinery in motion. Contemporary records show that he worked hard to promote better relations between the Town and University. He fully realised the valuable part the school could play in bringing this about. As a prominent citizen of Cambridge and as one who had twice filled the office of mayor and had been

[1] Martin Perse eventually became a Perse Fellow. He died in 1646 and by his will bequeathed a legacy to the Perse almswomen. The last kinsman of the Founder to be connected with the school was Thomas, son of Thomas Elwin, brother-in-law of Stephen Perse, who was admitted as free scholar in 1641.

sheriff of the county, he was in a position to interest influential people in the school. It is evident that Martin Perse performed his duties of trustee conscientiously. During part of each year he resided at Frating to manage the trust estates. The remainder of the year was spent at his house in Cambridge, and his close interest in the school is revealed in the care with which he nominated the free scholars, and selected boys of real ability to fill the vacancies on the Perse foundation at Caius.

Jeremy Taylor owed his nomination to a free scholar's place to Martin Perse. The future Bishop of Down and Connor was the son of a Cambridge barber, and baptised at Holy Trinity Church on August 15, 1613. He appears to have been one of the original free scholars,—in fact, he may have come with Lovering to the Perse from King's College School. He was, we are told, "ripe for the University afore custom would allow of his admittance." In 1626, when only thirteen years old, he proceeded to Caius, where he was on the nomination of Martin Perse elected a Perse Scholar. At the age of twenty he became a Fellow on the same foundation. As his biographer says, " he was a man before he was of age and knew little more of the state of childhood than its innocency and pleasantness."

Taylor's connection with his old school did not

end when he entered the University. After his election to a fellowship, he took pupils in accordance with the usual custom. Amongst these pupils were three Perse boys. One of these was a medical student named Edward Langsdale. There was a great sympathy between Taylor and this pupil, who was only six years his junior—a sympathy which ripened into life-long friendship. When, in 1635, Taylor was persuaded by Archbishop Laud to go to Oxford, Langsdale went with him. Four years later the tie between the two was made closer still by Taylor's marriage to Phoebe Langsdale, his pupil's sister.

In the case of another of his pupils, Taylor was able to repay a debt to a family to whom he owed much, for the boy in question was the younger Martin Perse. In the care which he bestowed on these three boys—and more especially the last mentioned—we can most certainly trace Taylor's gratitude for the early training which had laid in him "the good humour of a gentleman, the eloquence of an orator, the fancy of a poet, and the acuteness of a schoolman, the profoundness of a philosopher, the wisdom of a councillor, the sagacity of a prophet, the reason of an angel, and the piety of a saint."

CHAPTER III

THE CIVIL WAR PERIOD. (1636-52)

THE school remained under the care of Lovering and Martin Perse for the first eighteen years of its existence. Nothing better testifies to their conscientious attention to duty than the fact that in the troublous times, which were to follow, the Perse weathered storms in which shipwreck would have been the fate of a school less securely established. The connection between the school and both Master and executor came to an end before the Civil War. Death carried off Martin Perse in the April of 1636, whilst he was serving the office of Mayor.[1] At midsummer in the same year Lovering left Cambridge to become Master of Norwich Grammar School. At Norwich Lovering fully maintained the reputation which he had won at the Perse. He

---

[1] The Perse family continued to reside at Westwick in Cambridgeshire, where Martin Perse was lord of the manor. Valentine Perse sold this property some time after 1652. The last known member of the family was William Perse (formerly of Christ's), who died rector of West Heslerton, Yorks, about 1723.

earned golden opinions from his pupils. Under
his successor they looked back with regret on the
days when they were " wont to be made by Mr.
Loveringe Minerva's darlings," for their new
master, Mr. Mazey—a former Persean be it con-
fessed—suffered from the dread diseases known as
" desidia, chiragra, and podagra," and had reduced
his pupils to the intellectual miseries of " Vulcan's
servile bondslaves." [1]

On the death of the last survivor of the three
executors, the right of appointing the Master and
Usher was to devolve, in accordance with the terms
of the Founder's will, upon the Master and four
senior Fellows of Caius College. Both Cary (d. 1622)
and Spicer (d. 1629) had predeceased Martin Perse.
Caius College was, therefore, called upon to exercise
this right within three months of succession to the
trusteeship. It can hardly be said that their first
choice augured well for their conduct in the future.
Richard Watson (Master, 1636-41) was certainly
a distinguished scholar, but his appointment violated
the school ordinance prohibiting pluralism, for he
was a Fellow of Caius. The appointment afforded
a disastrous precedent for the future, and was not

[1] Lovering remained headmaster of Norwich until his death in
1667. Amongst his pupils at Norwich was the future Archbishop
Tenison.

justified in this particular instance by subsequent success. " A good scholar, but vain and conceited," was Antony à Wood's comment on Watson at a later date. To judge from Watson's own writings, Wood's criticism was sound. In his younger days he was certainly too self-centred to devote much energy to the management of the Perse. His attention was distracted by college and university matters. Besides holding a fellowship at Caius he undertook the duties of tutor and dean. In 1639 he combined with these the office of college lecturer in rhetoric. He was also much in request as a preacher of a highly polemical order. In justice to Watson, it should be recorded that he did take a personal interest in some of his pupils at the Perse, and acted as tutor to four of them when they entered Caius. Against this must, however, be set several very significant facts. At the time of his resignation the steady stream of boys proceeding from the Perse to the University had become reduced to a mere trickle ; boys were no longer attracted to the school from places beyond the immediate neighbourhood ; and last, but not least, no less than one-third of the free scholars' places were vacant when Watson left.[1]

[1] Watson was ejected from his fellowship at Caius in 1644 for preaching a sermon at Great St. Mary's Church " touching schism " (printed in 1642). He subsequently fled to the Continent. At the Restoration he was restored to his fellowship and became chaplain

Learning wisdom from the result of their previous transgression of the school ordinances, the Trustees conformed to the ordinances in appointing Watson's successor. At the same time they entered thoroughly into the spirit of the Founder's will by appointing a former Persean. Thomas Crabbe (Master, 1641-52) was the son of a Cambridge alderman, and had been a pupil of Lovering. He was the first and most successful of the three Masters who received their early education at the school. Ralph Harison, another Persean, was appointed Usher at the same time, and on his resignation three years later another old boy was appointed in the person of Robert Crayford. Thus a laudable attempt was made to foster a healthy feeling of *esprit de corps*, which, had it been permitted to continue, might well have brought the Perse to the forefront in the scholastic world. The experiment immediately proved successful. Indeed but for the patriotism of the masters the school might never have weathered the stormy decade which was now to begin.

to James, Duke of York. He died in 1685. Antony à Wood, in his *Athenae Oxonienses*, says that he was ejected from his Mastership at the Perse for his sermon "touching schism," and Cooper has repeated this statement in his *Annals of Cambridge*. The Perse Accounts, however, show that Watson had resigned from the Perse before the sermon was preached.

The coming of Crabbe was at once followed by an increase in the number of boys. During the first month of his Mastership no less than thirty-three free scholars were admitted. From the surviving sheets of a lost register we learn that between April, 1641, and July, 1649, there were no less than one hundred and twenty-seven entries—and this in spite of the fact that the country was filled with the alarums and excursions of the Civil War and that Cambridge suffered from recurring visitations of the plague. As many as twenty-three of these boys are known to have proceeded to the University, and of these seven ultimately became fellows of their colleges. Others, in later life, became prominent members of the Corporation of Cambridge. The boys were drawn from all classes. The great majority were the sons of tradesmen and college servants, and these figure largely amongst those who obtained university honours. The professional classes also sent their sons to the school. Two of the boys were the sons of Dr. Love, Master of Corpus, whose confidence in Crabbe is a notable tribute to the latter's ability. For a time, indeed, it looked as if the traditions of the Lovering régime would be revived in full. This hope was, however, not to be realised, but its non-fulfilment can in no way be imputed to Crabbe.

A few months after his appointment Crabbe received an Irish boy, named John Sterne, into the school. This boy had fled with his father from Drogheda on the outbreak of the Irish Rebellion.[1] As he received young Sterne into the school, Crabbe could not but have been impressed with the gloomy outlook in public affairs. The Irish Rebellion was but the prelude to more widespread strife. In the latter part of 1642 differences between King and Parliament came to a head, and bloodshed was inevitable. Adherents of both parties began to arm. Crabbe's old schoolfellow, John Pepys, attempted to smuggle arms into Cambridge for the use of the Royalists in the University. Only two chests of arms reached their destination. The remaining eight were seized owing to the vigilance of the member for the borough, Oliver Cromwell. In fact, the member for Cambridge was quick to secure East Anglia for Parliament. On an evening in March 1643, Lovering may well have seen his former Cambridge pupil, Tollemache Castell of Raveningham, brought by Cromwell a prisoner of war into Norwich after assisting his father in a vain attempt to raise the King's standard in Norfolk.

So far as Cambridge was concerned, the contest was soon decided. The town became the head-

[1] Entry in Sidney College Admission Register, October 3, 1645.

quarters of the Eastern Counties Association, of which Neville Butler, another of Crabbe's school-fellows, was a prominent member. Though alarms of threatened Royalist attacks were many, neither Cambridge nor its immediate neighbourhood was the scene of actual fighting. For a short time the Royalist sympathies of the University caused Parliament some anxiety, but in 1644 the Manchester Commissioners removed the most prominent opponents of Parliament from office, and after that year the Royalist element ceased to exist.

We know that Crabbe's sympathies were with the Royal party. At the Restoration he was rewarded by preferment in the Church and University. As Master of the Perse, however, Crabbe eschewed the political controversies of the time. The people of Cambridge were heart and soul for the Parliament. Amongst Crabbe's pupils were the sons of some of the stalwarts of the Parliamentary party. It speaks highly not only for Crabbe's political moderation but also for his reputation as a schoolmaster that he had the confidence of his fellow-townsmen, and that during this difficult period not a single allegation of " scandalousness " or " insufficiency " was ever made against him.

In spite of the Master's tact and moderation the Civil War was destined to affect the fortunes of the

Perse very seriously. The county of Essex suffered severely from the heavy taxation imposed upon it. The Frating tenants were considerable sufferers, and professed themselves unable to pay their rents. Owing to the distance and the unsettled state of the country, the Trustees found it impossible to collect all their rents, even supposing the money had been forthcoming. At Christmas, 1643, the income of the trust had almost vanished. Retrenchment alone would save the situation. Accordingly it was agreed to reduce the salaries of all officers connected with the trust. The Master and Usher found their stipends reduced temporarily by one-half, and had to rest content with vague promises of receiving their arrears in full when finances would permit of it.

Both Crabbe and his Usher, Robert Crayford, stuck loyally to their posts during the next four critical years. The year 1644 perhaps saw matters looking their blackest. Only four free scholars were admitted. Owing to the disturbed state of the country hardly a single boarder attended the school, and the masters were thus deprived of one possible means of recouping themselves for their lost income. To add to these troubles, in the autumn a storm damaged the roof and chimneys of the school, and the cost of repairs absorbed a large part of the remaining scanty income of the trust.

In 1645, thanks to the energy of the masters, the horizon began to look brighter. The entry rose to eleven, to rise again to seventeen in the following year. In 1647 the two masters received part of their back pay. Twelve months later the remaining arrears were paid off, and the Master and Usher were once more allowed their full stipends. The outlook brightened generally. The threatened disaster had been averted, and the school saved by the disinterested patriotism of two of its old boys.

With the crisis past, it might have been expected that Crabbe would be allowed to govern the school in peace. Unhappily for him this was not to be. In 1649 the Manchester Commissioners appointed William Dell to the mastership of Caius on the ejection of Thomas Batchcroft, who was a Royalist. As Master of Caius Dell became ex-officio chairman of the Perse trustees. He had formerly been chaplain to the New Model Army, and in religious matters was a man of few sympathies and many antipathies. His claim to celebrity does not, however, rest upon the eccentricity of his religious views, but upon the very modern theories on education propounded in his *Right Reformation of Learning*.

The greater part of Dell's book is devoted to an attack on the monopoly of university teaching then enjoyed by Cambridge and Oxford. For us, how-

OLD SCHOOL IN FREE SCHOOL LANE (INTERIOR), AS USED FOR THE
MEETING OF THE BRITISH ASSOCIATION, 1845

ever, the main interest lies in the first portion of this book, which advocates a complete reformation of the grammar school system. Dell insists that the education of youth is a matter for the State and recommends the establishment of schools throughout the country, not only in towns but also in villages. In these schools he would have a more extended range of subjects, as well as a greater discrimination in their treatment. The instructors should first teach their pupils " to read their native tongue, which they know without understanding : and then presently as they understand, bring them to read the Holy Scriptures ; which though for the present they understand not, yet they may through the blessing of God, come to understand them afterwards." In towns, the scholars should be taught " also the Latin and Greek tongues, and the Hebrew also, which is the easiest of them all, and ought to be in great account with us for the Old Testament's sake." But a very careful selection is to be made of the classical authors.

" My counsel is that they learn the Latin and Greek tongues especially from Christians, and so without the lies, fables, follies, vanities, lust, pride, revenge, etc. of the heathens ; especially seeing that neither their words nor their phrases are meet for Christians to take into their mouths : and most necessary it is, that Christians should forget the names of their gods and muses, which were but devils and damned creatures, and all their mythology and fabulous inventions, and let them all go to Satan from whence they came."

Ovid and Virgil are thus consigned to perdition, and practically every writer who has hitherto been studied is to be excluded from the syllabus of the reformed grammar school.

Dell had a good opportunity of putting his reforms to a practical test at the Perse. He was, it is true, frequently absent from Cambridge, and cannot have very actively superintended the carrying out of his theories. Nevertheless, we know that he interested himself in other matters connected with the school, and can hardly doubt that as a soi-disant educationalist he availed himself of the opportunity of experimenting along the lines of his theories. Crabbe probably offered little opposition to some of Dell's innovations, but he was thoroughly conservative at heart, and must have regarded with misgiving the drastic changes proposed in the teaching of classics. Dell's known eccentricity of character and impracticability of temper made even men of advanced views chary of endorsing the sentiments of the *Right Reformation of Learning*.

Under the circumstances, it was to be expected that differences would arise between Crabbe and Dell. At Michaelmas, 1652, we find the post of Master of the Perse School vacant. Crabbe's departure was obviously unexpected, for the Trustees were momentarily at a loss to find a successor. Furthermore the resignation cannot have been altogether voluntary, for Crabbe held no other post in view when he left.[1] It is not unreasonable to suppose that owing to friction with Dell he had found his position insufferable, and had been induced or compelled to resign. His past sacrifices for the school had merited freedom from such molestation, and our sympathies must be with him rather than with Dell. Enlightened as many of Dell's views were, it must not be forgotten that his own age regarded him as an eccentric and a crank. It was Crabbe's misfortune that such a man came across his path.

Indirectly Crabbe's retirement was due to the revolution in the world of politics. Other Perseans were more directly victims of the troubles of the Civil War and of the passing of the Act of Uniformity in 1662. They were to be found in both camps, and included soldiers and clergy. Reference has already been made to the parts played by John Pepys, Tollemache Castell, and Neville Butler in

[1] Crabbe held no ecclesiastical or scholastic appointment until the Restoration. He was then elected a Fellow of Caius. He was ordained in 1670 and became rector of Hardwick, Norfolk, where he died in 1680.

the early days of the Civil War.   In the later stages of the war we find others fighting on the Royalist side.   John, second Viscount Chaworth, garrisoned his house at Wiverton, Notts, for the King, and later shared in the defence of Newark, for which acts his estates were sequestrated by Parliament.   Edmund Thorold [1] was also one of the defenders of Newark.   Richard Naylor of Godmanchester was another active Royalist, and at the Restoration was proposed as one of the knights of the intended Order of the Royal Oak.   Jeremy Taylor was at one time a chaplain to the Royalist Army, and suffered imprisonment for the part he played.   A similar fate befell Robert Dixon, who in his own time had a considerable reputation as a writer of theological treatises.[2]   James Lukyn, vicar of Puddletown, Dorset, was sequestrated from his living, but " lived to be restored and died the faithful pastor of his church."   In a younger generation, Thomas Wilson of Caius College allowed his perfervid royalism to get him into trouble with the Vice-chancellor, who in 1649 suspended him from his degree " for drinking a health to the King and confusion to Tom [sc. Fairfax]."

[1] Fellow of St. John's College, Cambridge, 1634 ; Prebendary of Lincoln, 1660.

[2] A full account of Dixon is given in the *Dictionary of National Biography*.

The Act of Uniformity drove more than one Persean out of his living. Amongst the Independents can be mentioned John Yaxley,[1] Andrew Thomaton,[2] and James Thelwall.[3] Thomas Ellis was deprived of the living of Lopham, Norfolk, for holding Anabaptist tenets. Thomas Owen, rector of Bramfield, Herts, signed the Solemn League and Covenant, and for that reason was deprived in 1660 : subsequently he conformed, and died vicar of Sundridge in Kent. Richard Laurence, a man " humble and inoffensive in his carriage, and generally well spoken of," was ejected in 1662 from the rectory of Trunch, Norfolk, and for a time was pastor to the Independent congregation at Amsterdam.

[1] Rector of Kibworth, Leicester.   [2] Rector of Scrivelsby, Lincs.
[3] Vicar of Whiston, Yorks.

CHAPTER IV

THE COMMONWEALTH AND RESTORATION PERIOD.
(1652-87)

WHEN Dell and his colleagues got rid of Crabbe, they had no nominee to put in his place. They deferred making any new appointment for four months. During the Michaelmas term the Usher, Crayford, undertook the entire management of the school, and was allowed fourteen pounds for his pains. At Christmas, 1652, the Trustees appointed George Griffith of Queens' to the vacant post. The new Master was a native of London, and had originally been a member of Emmanuel, Dell's former college and a stronghold of Puritanism. In the early days of 1645 the Manchester Commissioners put him into a fellowship at Queens'. His previous record was therefore sufficient to enable him to find favour with Dell and his co-trustees.

As can be gathered from subsequent events, Robert Crayford was bitterly disappointed that the Mastership was not conferred on him. It is not altogether clear why the Trustees did not promote him in view of his past services to the school. At a later date they declared that he was ineligible, because in 1651 he had accepted the curacy of Haslingfield, " wherebye ye Ushers place was much deserted." According to the school ordinances this certainly was a bar to his promotion, but by the same ordinances he was equally ineligible for the post of Usher. The Trustees had no right to retain him in one post and debar him from the other. Furthermore, if the ordinances were to be enforced against Crayford, it was very unjust that they were not made to operate against Griffith, who at the time of his appointment still held a fellowship at Queens'.

Whatever sympathy may be felt for Crayford in his disappointment is altogether alienated by his subsequent conduct. The new Master's position could not have been easy under any circumstances. Crayford did his utmost to make it difficult. On October 20th, 1653, in defiance of both Trustees and Master he intruded seven boys into the school, who were ineligible for free scholars' places. It is hardly credible that such an act of defiance should have been possible—still less credible that the Trustees should have been unable to remove the intruders at once—yet such was the case. These seven boys frequented the school during the whole of the Michaelmas term, and did not leave until Crayford himself left.[1]

On finding that he could defy the governors' orders, Crayford went still further. Other acts of unruliness followed, culminating in open insubordination. In the words of one of the scandalised governors,

" Before all ye Schollers he in a most violent manner made an assault upon George Griffith, he the saide George in the peace of God & the publicke peace then & there beinge : and said also scandalous, opprobrious, & reproachfull words following to Griffith, to witt, you are a strikinge knave : you come to steale away my due : I will take you a kicke on the britch & tred in your feete."

Insubordination was followed by acts of scandalous barbarity towards the boys. Several instances of his cruelty are recorded, and these leave behind them the impression that the Usher was not altogether sane. We read, for instance, of

" One Thomas Peters, whom ye saide Robert Crayford wrung by both his eares in y^at violent manner that one of his eares was cruelly torne both skinn and grissle & almost went from his head : ye said Thomas Peters goeinge home to his mother Katherine Peters house in Cambridge with his eare soe torne & bleedinge to her great affrightment,

[1] The following information is given in the Sidney Admission Register, under the date August 22, 1657, concerning John Chishull, who is mentioned as being one of the intruded scholars : " institutus literis grammaticis primo quidem Cantabrigiae nostrae in schola Perciana *sed non amplius quatuor menses.*"

the blood runninge downe ye body of the said Thomas Peters from his head unto his feet.

"And ye saide Robt. Crayford did in such unmercifull and cruell manner whip one John Spratford, one of ye Schollers in ye free grammer schoole of Cambridge aforesaide, y^{at} his body was sor gashed and torne by his cruell stripes, that he could scarce indure to lay himselfe downe in his bed at night. And after complaint thereof made to the said Robert Crayford by John Spratford, of the Towne of Cambridge, father of the said John Spratford, ye said John was still from tyme to tyme so harshly dealt with by the said Robert Crayford, that the said John Spratford was constrained att length to take his said sonne from ye said free schoole & put to him to a private grammer schoole in Cambridge.

"And ye said Robt. Crayford did smite one Edward Webb, being one of ye Schollers in ye free grammer schoole, in a most violent manner upon his jawes & beat hym downe with his head against a wooden forme. Webb riseing upp again, Crayford smote him ye second tyme in like manner in soe much y^{at} his head and jawes were soe bruised, y^{at} the saide Edward was in very great danger of death. Edward Webbe, father of ye saide Edward, being a Chirurgeon, besides his own skill in Chirurgerie, wh. he used for his sonne his care, took the advise of one Doctor Eade, a knowne & skilfull Physician, who gave ye sonne over fearinge y^{at} he was not curable: yet it pleased God y^{at} after five weekes he did some what recover, but is to this day by the cruell usage of Crayford soe much disabled in his speech & also in his memorie, y^{at} his father to his great greife was necessitated to divert him from ye way of a scholler to a seruilar imploym^t."

Obviously such acts as these did a great deal of harm to the school. The time had come for the Trustees

to dispense with the Usher's services.   Accordingly
at Christmas, 1653, Crayford was dismissed, and
his place given to John Felton, Fellow of Caius.

But matters did not end here.   Crayford was
occupying the Usher's house, and he refused to
surrender it.   His dismissal aroused the indignation
of certain townspeople, " more," we are told, " in
opposition to the college [sc. Caius] than in friendship to him."   It is well-nigh inconceivable that
after his recent conduct Crayford could have found
many sympathisers in Cambridge : yet sympathisers
he undoubtedly had.   Without their assistance he
could not have defied the Trustees for so long a
period as he did.   They encouraged him to contest
the decision of the Trustees and to apply for a
mandamus for his restitution.   A writ of mandamus
was in due course issued.   With unconscious irony
it declared that ever since his appointment to the
post of Usher, Robert Crayford had " behaved &
governed himselfe welle, quietly, soberly, &
honestly," and commanded the Trustees to restore
him to his post, unless good cause could be shown
to the contrary.

The Trustees at once entered a defence, and Dell
deposed to all Crayford's past offences.   Crayford
was determined to vindicate himself at all costs and
to obtain full compensation for " the manifest

wearinge of his creditt Estate." The Trustees were equally determined not to have him back again, and went to considerable expense to fight the matter out. The legal proceedings, therefore, had to take their usual course. The writ had been issued on February 13th, 1653-4, but it was not until the Trinity term of 1655 that the action came before the Court of the Upper Bench, as the King's Bench was then styled. At the hearing Crayford's counsel made a strong appeal for an order of restitution, but the Lord Chief Justice declined to intervene after learning that Crayford had " much abused himself." He recommended the parties to refer their differences to the justices of assize, one of whom, Oliver St. John, was then Chancellor of Cambridge University.

All these proceedings had been costly, as is shown by numerous items in the trust accounts for this period. The trust funds were still in low water, and a further prosecution of the quarrel would have involved a heavy drain on an already impoverished income. There were also considerations of an even more pressing nature. Crayford had not been evicted from the Usher's house. He still defied the Trustees in the very precincts of the school, and declined to surrender any of the school property, which had come into his hands as Usher. He endeavoured to be thoroughly offensive to Griffith.

Apparently the unfortunate Master had on more than one occasion to submit to insulting language of a nature very similar to that already recorded. Furthermore, Crayford's friends endeavoured to establish a boycott of the school.

Obviously it was imperative to get the ex-Usher out of the way at all costs. The fortunes of the school were in jeopardy, and the situation was growing daily more intolerable for the unfortunate Griffith. The Trustees decided to come to terms rather than prosecute the quarrel to a costly victory. Accordingly they abandoned the lawsuit, and effected a compromise with Crayford. On April 17, 1656, the parties entered into a composition. Crayford renounced all claims to the post and emoluments of Usher. In consideration therefor he was allowed to occupy the Usher's house for one year on his undertaking to " demean himselfe fairely, soberly, & inoffensively to the Master & Usher of the schoole for the tyme beinge." Apparently Crayford abided faithfully by the agreement, for there was no more trouble. At the latter end of 1657 he left Cambridge to take the living of East Grinstead in Sussex, where he died in 1683. His was an ill-balanced mind, and some of his acts savoured of madness. His two years' defiance of the Trustees and Master showed a dogged pertinacity in fighting a desperate cause, which calls forth a regret that it was not put to a better use. Whilst we condemn his scandalous barbarity and insubordination, we must not forget his disinterested patriotism at a critical moment in the school's history. Twenty years later his son returned to Cambridge, and was received into his father's old college at Caius. As a Perse Scholar and Perse Fellow he cleared the name of the obloquy brought upon it by his father's conduct.

Though Crayford was gone, Griffith was by no means out of troubled waters. The dispute might be settled, but the ill feeling aroused thereby did not easily die down. A section of the townspeople still bore a grudge against the school, and could still boycott the Perse by sending boys to private schools in the town. Fortunately, Griffith was not wanting in tact, and in time all hostility disappeared. The first step taken to allay ill feeling was the resignation of the Usher. Felton's appointment had been the bone of contention from the very outset. His position was by no means enviable, and, as the salary attached to his post was diminishing, there was little inducement for him to remain. It was probably with very little reluctance that he resigned at the Michaelmas following Crayford's departure.[1]

[1] Felton apparently took an interest in his pupils at the Perse, for he acted as tutor to two of them after their admission at Caius.

We can trace the hand of the Master of Caius in the appointment of Felton's successor. John Boult supplied " the vacancies of prayers in chapel " at Caius College during this period, and was regarded as a Puritan in religion. He would, therefore, be considered eminently fitted to assist in furtherance of the projects set forth in the *Right Reformation of Learning*. The new Usher did not, however, stay longer at the school than twelve months.[1] His immediate successors were William Henry Rixe (Usher, 1657-67), William Peters (Usher, 1667-76), and Edward Sparkes (Usher, 1676-87). All three had originally been pupils of Griffith. In each case, however, the appointment was made in violation of the school ordinances, for each of them held either a fellowship or ecclesiastical preferment simultaneously with the post of Usher. In the cases of Peters and Rixe little harm was done thereby, for both were able men.[2] Nevertheless, the bad precedent of Watson's time was revived, and was to have a serious effect on the fortunes of the school before the century was out.

[1] Like Felton Boult seems to have taken an interest in his pupils at the Perse, for he also acted as tutor to two Perseans on their admission at Caius, one of them being John Spratford (cf. p. 57).

[2] Rixe subsequently became Master of Saffron Walden. From the Sidney Admission Register (May 5, 1669) we learn that he took at least one of his pupils from the Perse to Saffron Walden.

So long as Dell remained Master of Caius, Griffith's position could not have been altogether easy. The theories of the *Right Reformation of Learning* were still very dear to their author. The general public, on the other hand, regarded both author and theories with suspicion. Griffith, therefore, had a difficult course to steer, if he desired to placate both parties. Fortunately, both for himself and the Perse, he had both moderation and discernment. Without alienating public opinion by radical innovation, he at the same time managed to avoid Crabbe's fate. At the Restoration this policy of moderation was justified. Dell ceased to be Master of Caius, and saw all his handiwork undone. Griffith was left undisturbed. His views on political and religious matters were not extreme, and must have caused bitter disappointment to the " outed " Master of Caius. Amongst the collection of verses composed by members of the University to welcome Charles II. on his return from exile we find a contribution by Griffith. With equally deep regret Dell must have read two other contributions from the ex-Ushers, Felton and Boult.

After 1660 religious and political controversies ceased to play any part in the history of the school. Griffith was left to rule the Perse undisturbed by external events. The rest of his Mastership was comparatively peaceful. One event did, however, for the moment, interrupt the even tenour of school life. This was the plague. Throughout its history Cambridge was a frequent sufferer from pestilence. In 1630 the town suffered from an exceptionally severe visitation, which for a time must have completely arrested the progress of the school. During Crabbe's Mastership the plague recurred in Cambridge almost annually. To judge, however, from the admission register for that period these visitations were regarded with comparative equanimity. Except perhaps for a period between April, 1643, and April, 1644, when no admissions are recorded, the regular routine of school life was not interrupted. The visitations of 1665 and the following year were far more serious matters. At Cambridge the plague proved most fatal in the autumn of 1666, when it claimed victims amongst the families of several boys then attending the school, and no doubt amongst the boys themselves. Griffith, apparently, had no alternative but to close the school for the time being. Some Perse boys were sent to neighbouring towns until the plague had abated. Edmund Ivory, for instance, was sent to Bury St. Edmunds and attended the school there, returning to the Perse when the visitation was past. By the spring of 1667 the pestilence at Cambridge had run its course.

Thereafter the continuity of school life was never again interrupted by plague.

Meanwhile, through all the vicissitudes of politics, lawsuits, and pestilence, Griffith steadily increased his reputation as a schoolmaster. Parents, including persons of high social standing, sent their sons from all parts of the country to the Perse. Sir Ralph Hare of Stow Bardolph, Norfolk, sent his son Thomas.[1] Another pupil, Edward Russell of Chippenham, came of a family closely allied by marriage with that of Cromwell.[2] But the best evidence of Griffith's ability is revealed in the remarkable number of boys sent up to the University. We can trace sixty-seven entering six different colleges in Cambridge, and of this number no less than fifteen obtained fellowships. One, Christopher Greene, became Regius Professor of Physic, and proved his versatility by also holding the lectureships in Greek and Ethics at Caius.

The most distinguished of all Griffith's pupils was undoubtedly Sir Robert Tabor.[3] After leaving

---

[1] Thomas Hare succeeded to his father's baronetcy in 1671 whilst still at the Perse. He was a patron of the engraver, David Loggan, and represented Norfolk in Parliament 1685-88.

[2] The father, Sir Francis Russell, was one of Cromwell's major-generals and a member of his upper house. His eldest son married the Protector's daughter.

[3] He was grandson of James Tabor, the well-known University Registrary. The Tabor family had a close connection with the

school, Tabor was apprenticed to an apothecary in Cambridge. During his apprenticeship he discovered a satisfactory method of administering quinine in cases of fever. The opportunity for proving the value of his discovery came in 1678, when he managed by his remedy to save the life of Charles II., who in gratitude knighted him. His reputation spread to the continent. Louis XIV. sent for him to attend the Dauphin, and later he became medical adviser to the Queen Consort of Spain.

Later in life another of Griffith's pupils made his mark as a commentator and as a pioneer of the evangelical movement. This was William Burkitt, concerning whose school career we have something more than the usual information. Whilst a boy " he was endowed with a very Tenacious Memory, which through the happiness of a good Education was made a Cabinet for Jewels, a Repository of Scripture and Catechism." Even at school he was of a deeply serious turn of mind. It was at the Perse that his vocation came to him. " While I continued at School in Cambridge," he tells us, " it

Perse in its early days. Sir Robert's uncle, James, was a boy at the school. Matthew Whynne, who married the Registrary's daughter and succeeded his father-in-law in his office, was contemporary with this second James at the Perse. Sir Robert Tabor's brother John was also a pupil of Griffith.

PERSE SCHOOL CHRISTMAS ANNUAL, 1874

pleased God to visit me with the Small-Pox, but very favourably, and, as I hope, in great mercy, laying the Foundation of my Spiritual Health in that sickness, working, as I hope, a prevailing thorough change in the very Frame and disposition of my Soul." [1]

As the school was in financial straits during the whole of his Mastership, Griffith's success is the more creditable. The end of the Civil War did not bring the hoped-for improvement of the Frating property. Moreover, whilst the trust income diminished, expenditure increased. Crayford's action had been costly. There were other heavy legal expenses incidental to the conveyance of the trust property from Thomas Batchcroft, the last surviving feofee under the Founder's will, to the Master and four senior fellows of Caius. In addition to law costs, there were considerable outgoings for the upkeep of the fabric of the school. The trust accounts for 1668 record the payment of ten pounds to " one Perse a relation of Dr. Perses by the Colledgorder." It is indeed to be hoped that the recipient was worthy of his family, for it was not the time to throw away money in mistaken charity. To meet all these outgoings retrenchment was

[1] A full account of Burkitt is given in the *Dictionary of National Biography*.

practised at the expense of the unfortunate Master and Usher, who only on rare occasions received their full salaries. In 1678 Griffith's stipend was cut down to £32 and that of his Usher to £16.

Griffith had a private income, and his heart was in his work. He was not, therefore, to be deterred by inadequate payment. He held the Mastership for thirty-four years. The beginning had been stormy : the end came amid peace. Nearly half a century had passed since the day on which he first came as a stranger to the University. Since then his whole life had been centred in Cambridge. In his early days he had been the subject of quarrels and much bitterness. By his own effort he lived down all antipathies, and gained the universal respect of his fellow townsmen. In the parish of St. Edward's he was till the end a leading figure—full of kindly thought for his humbler neighbours. The autumn of 1686 found him in failing health. On Michaelmas day he was unable to go to Caius College to receive his stipend, for the payment is recorded, but the customary receipt is absent. He just outlived the year. At length, on January 6th, 1687, his long and useful life ended.

Griffith's will bears the date November 12th, 1686. He left legacies to the poor of St. Edward's parish and the Perse almswomen, as well as one hundred pounds to Hobson's Charity " for the setting the poore on work." But to us the most interesting legacy is the sum of one hundred pounds bequeathed to the Master and four Senior Fellows of Caius " to be by them employed to the best advantage for a supplement to the revenues of Dr. Stephen Perses Free School in Cambridge." To this benefaction his executrix adds certain of his " goods and utensills of household stuff " to the value of fifty pounds for the free use of his successors in the Mastership.

In 1841, when the school ordinances were re-modelled, the revisers fittingly perpetuated this bequest by making the following order :

" In the prayers to be used at the times that the Scholars do break up school before the vacations and the times they come together again after the said vacations, some mention shall be made of Dr. Perse the founder, and Mr. George Griffith and others the benefactors of the School, with giving thanks for the same."

CHAPTER V

DECLINE AND FALL (1687-1787)

In his diary Alderman Samuel Newton gives the following record of certain events connected with the Perse, which occurred in the early days of 1687 :

" 6th January being Thursday about 6 of the clock in the afternoone dyed Mr George Griffith Schoolemaster of the Freeschoole in Cambridge. Hee was laid in the ground in St Edwards Chancel on Saturday night following between 8 and 9 of the clock. His funeral was on Tuesday in the afternoone beinge the 11th day of January.

" 9th January being Sunday after Evening Chappell at Caius College was Mr Edward Sparkes admitted Master of Dr Perses Free Schoole in Cambridge in the roome of Mr. Griffith deceased."

The haste with which the Trustees made their appointment might well be called indecent. Griffith's obsequies had not yet been performed, when his successor was appointed. A general indifference to the duties of their trust—symptomatic of worse to come—could be the only reason for their conduct. There was nothing in the character or ability of the new Master to justify the extraordinary haste with which the appointment was made. As free scholar, Perse scholar at Caius, Usher, and Master of the school, Edward Sparkes was connected with the Perse foundation for sixty-five years, and few have so ill repaid their alma mater. As Usher during Griffith's declining years, he had apparently been more or less in sole charge of the school, and there had been a general falling off in the number of the pupils. Furthermore, in 1686 Sparkes had violated the school ordinances by accepting the living of Shepreth and, notwith-standing, had been allowed to remain at the Perse.

The financial difficulties confronting the school at this time might well have discouraged an abler man than Sparkes. After 1693 Griffith's bequest brought in an annual sum of £4 10s., which was employed to supplement the masters' stipends, but the falling off in the remainder of the trust revenues continued. In 1688 both Master and Usher found their salaries reduced by one-half. The salaries remained at these figures until 1716, when they were raised to £30 and £15 respectively. It was not until 1735 that the full statutable incomes were once more paid to the two masters. The self-sacrifice of Crabbe was a tradition of the past of which Sparkes was oblivious. Being utterly devoid of ambition, he was content to remain as he was, to obtain what salary he could, and to do the least possible required for the earning of it.

During the first ten years following Griffith's death a fair sprinkling of boys proceeded from the Perse to the University, but most of them were unremarkable and none of them subsequently distinguished themselves either in the academic or other spheres of life. Such credit as may be due for their success was perhaps as much due to the Ushers as the Master. Robert Pate, Sparkes' first Usher, was certainly a man of some ability, and subsequently became Master of Norwich School.[1] His stay at the Perse, however, was limited to a single term. At the end of that period we find him keeping a private school in Cambridge. Several boys, who were originally at the Perse, attended this school—a circumstance which clearly indicates that all was not well at the Perse.

On Pate's resignation the Trustees for once broke with the old custom of appointing Caius men to the post of Usher. Their choice fell on James Gill of Pembroke Hall,[2] but on his death in 1692 they reverted to their former practice, appointing Thomas Inyon, who was already a Fellow of Caius. There-

[1] Pate had been a boy at the Perse under Griffith.
[2] He was a native of Cambridge and perhaps educated at the Perse.

after, until the nineteenth century had begun, not a single appointment was made from outside of Caius College, and the majority of those appointed were Fellows of the College. It is not surprising, therefore, to discover that at the opening of the eighteenth century the Perse had ceased to be the leading school in the town, having given place to King's College School.

The year 1703 saw the establishment of charity schools in Cambridge.[1] Their establishment had a disastrous effect on the fortunes of the Perse. The children were, it is true, drawn from the humblest class and received the most elementary education. Nevertheless, in bygone days some of the ablest Perseans had been born of relatively poor parents. The teaching Sparkes gave offered little prospect of much advancement in life, and as the charity schools provided a sound utilitarian training, the humbler townspeople after 1703 ceased to send their boys to the Perse. Thus the school practically lost an important class, from which had sprung Jeremy Taylor and others of the ablest and most distinguished of its past pupils.[2]

---

[1] Now known as the Old Schools.

[2] A charity school was established at Trumpington in 1679 by a certain William Austin. Between 1687 and 1836 not a single record can be found of a Trumpington boy attending the Perse school.

With rivals in the field, the Perse required an Usher of some ability and character to supplement the mediocre talents of Sparkes. The least likely appointment to check the decay now setting in was that made in 1704 on Inyon's retirement. The Trustees could think of no more suitable person than the headmaster's own son. Brought up under the uninspiring tutelage of his father, his whole life confined within the narrow limits of his native town, the younger Sparkes entirely lacked that originality which alone could infuse new life into the school. He was a mere replica of the headmaster. For eighteen years the school was allowed to stagnate under this family arrangement. The monotony of perpetual deterioration was only broken when the son violated the school ordinances by accepting a living in Hertfordshire. His pluralism was tolerated for two years. At length, on his appointment in 1722 to the living of Ugley in Essex, either his conscience or that of the Trustees became somewhat tardily reproachful, and the post of Usher became vacant.

The elder Sparkes was now bordering on seventy and required a competent assistant to manage the school. Neither of his last two Ushers can be described as competent. Joseph Brett (Usher, 1722-24) certainly was not without ability. He subsequently became Master of Wymondham and Scarning Schools. But his methods of enforcing discipline were too brutal even for a generation not over squeamish in such matters. He was dismissed from Scarning for acts of gross cruelty to the children of the parish. Brett's successor, Daniel Munnings (Usher, 1724-27), had not even the merits of Brett. As Cole informs us, he was a spendthrift and " soon wasted his wife's fortune and died insolvent."

In 1727, Sparkes died suddenly at Shepreth,[1] at the age of seventy-three. After his forty years' rule the state of the Perse was indeed deplorable. Boys no longer proceeded from the school to the University. In fact, the numbers attending the school were so few that the Trustees considered the services of a second Master superfluous. For the time being, Munnings was placed in sole charge and allowed to draw the salaries of both Master and Usher.

An effort was made to deal with the situation six months later, when Munnings resigned. The Trustees, however, again resorted to their old practice of appointing Fellows of their own college, choosing Nathaniel Saltier as Master and Henry Goodall as Usher. There is little to be said

[1] St. Edward's Parish Register, May 24, 1727.

concerning Saltier's Mastership (1728-32). The school remained in the same state as in the latter days of Sparkes. The Bishop of Ely found only ten scholars in the school during a visitation of his diocese in 1731.[1] Even the confined premises in Free School Lane provided more than ample accommodation for this small number. Saltier realised this, and decided to eke out his very inadequate salary by letting the school. The buildings had ceased to be used as a school before 1731, for in that year the governors paid Mr. Jacob Butler of Barnwell Abbey a fee of one guinea " for pleading y[t] y[e] Freeschool should not be assessed to y[e] rates,"—an item which shows that the school was then occupied as a dwelling house or workshop. As a matter of fact, it is known who was Saltier's tenant. He was a certain Bernard Turner, who, besides being organist of St. John's, carried on the business of organ builder in the town. He occupied one of the two masters' houses, and used the school room as his workshop. In a note on Turner, Cole tells us that " in the schole I saw several of his organs, harpsichords, and spinets ; and I suppose he used it as his workshop, the schole having been neglected there many years : though when I first went to the University there was a flourishing schole."

[1] Add. MS. 7827, p. 89.

To judge from the practice of one of his successors, Saltier probably retained the Master's house for his own use. His few pupils must have been taught there or else in his college rooms.

In 1732 Saltier resigned and was succeeded by his Usher, Henry Goodall (Master, 1732-50). The new Master has best been described by Cole :

" He was of a mould framed by Nature, education, and constitution to be a bishop's chaplain : all humbleness, obsequiousness, flattery, and distance. The bishop [sc. of Ely] bred him up to the trade, in which he succeeded very well, . . . tho' to do him justice . . ., a very honest, sober, good-tempered man."

Goodall gained notoriety as a pluralist in an age of pluralism. He attached himself to the person of Sir Thomas Gooch, Master of Caius and Bishop of Bristol, Norwich, and Ely successively. There is no doubt that he succeeded very well at the trade. When Gooch, as ex-officio chairman of the Trustees, secured the Mastership of the Perse for his chaplain, Goodall was already a Fellow of Caius. In 1742 his patron obtained the living of Mattishall in Norfolk for him by an act of gross jobbery.[1] Five

---

[1] The Master and Fellows of Caius were the patrons of the living, but the Fellows did not want to present Goodall. Being fully aware of this fact, Gooch as Master of Caius declined to convene a college meeting. The appointment therefore lapsed to the Bishop of the diocese, who was none other than Gooch himself. Goodall was then appointed forthwith.

years later he was given the two livings of Bixley and Framlingham Earl in the same county, and twelve months later became Archdeacon of Suffolk. During the whole of this period he remained Master of the Perse.

As Goodall spent most of his time in attendance on his patron, the school was left to the care of his Ushers,[1] who, fortunately, were not so neglectful of their duties as the Master. Almost for the first time since the days of Griffith boys came to the school from places beyond the immediate neighbourhood, and once more a few Perseans proceeded to the University. Of the three Ushers responsible for this recovery Charles Davy (Usher, 1747-51) deserves more than passing reference. Later in life he published *Letters addressed chiefly to a Young Gentleman* (1787) and several other treatises on education, which have obtained a place for him in the *Dictionary of National Biography*. In his *Letters* he advocates the introduction of more mathematical and scientific training into school teaching, and attacks the old grammar school system with some vigour.

---

[1] James Willson (Usher 1732-40), Robert Goodrich (Usher 1740-47), and Charles Davy (Usher 1747-51). Of these Goodrich is remembered as the dean who quarrelled with and earned the life-long respect of the future Lord Chancellor Thurlow at the time when the latter was a turbulent Perse Scholar of Caius.

" I have ever been of opinion," he writes, " that giving up ten or twelve years of human life to two dead languages are more than we can afford.   In the number of young gentlemen of fortune, who are educated at our best public schools, scarce one in five hundred, perhaps, proves a very considerable classic scholar, and what with the neglect of science amongst those few, and that small attention which is paid to their religious principles, a greater part of them turn mere classic writers only."

The foregoing opinions were apparently the result of reflection in the retirement of the Norfolk rectory in which Davy ended his days.   There is nothing to show that he put his theories into practice at the Perse.   Indeed, from what little is known of his career as a schoolmaster, it would appear that he did not rise superior to his own times.   Like so many of his predecessors, he violated the school ordinances by combining his duties at the Perse with that of serving the curacy of Stow in Norfolk.   For us the interest of Davy's *Letters* lies in the fact that the Young Gentleman to whom they were addressed was his own son, who forty years later had the opportunity as Master of the Perse of putting his father's theories into practice.

Throughout Goodall's time the numbers attending the school must have been very small.   The organ-builder was still permitted to occupy the schoolhouse and one of the masters' houses.   An incident, which is recorded in the life of Christopher Smart, shows the insignificance to which the Perse had sunk.   At this date, Smart, who was afterwards to be known to fame for his *Song to David*, was a Fellow of Pembroke and was scandalizing the whole University by his levity and numerous escapades. In April, 1747, he shocked the whole academic world by proposing to stage a play of his own composition, entitled *A Trip to Cambridge*. Dramatic performances had gone out of vogue at Cambridge long before this date, and Smart had difficulty in finding a place wherein to stage his play. Seeing the schoolhouse deserted by its masters and Scholars he applied for the use of the premises.   His request was, however, refused, and eventually the performance took place in the hall of Pembroke.

After holding the Mastership for eighteen years, Goodall resigned, and his place was taken by Roger Sturgeon (Master, 1750-59).   The new Master appears to have been the last to have resided in Free School Lane for many years to come.   He held two livings—Waterbeach in Cambridgeshire and Hardmead in Buckinghamshire—but neither of these were rich.   Although a scholar of some ability, academic preferment never came his way. He had a wife and family to maintain on a very inadequate income, and in the end, as Cole informs us, " died very poor." Nevertheless, for his times Sturgeon was extremely conscientious. His parishioners at Hardmead no doubt learnt the evils of absenteeism, but he was scrupulous in the performance of his duties at Waterbeach and at the Perse. At the school he evidently made a struggle to remedy the neglect of the past. A few more boys were sent to the University, the most conspicuous being Henry Turner, who was the son of Sturgeon's tenant and subsequently became a Fellow of St. John's.

Sturgeon died at his house in Free School Lane in 1759. His pathetic struggle against poverty showed how impossible it was at this date to expect a master to devote his entire energies to his school when paid the utterly inadequate salary of forty pounds. It is not surprising, therefore, to find that in the next eight years four Masters were appointed in rapid succession.[1] The meagre stipends of the Master and Usher had to be augmented by work outside the school, which prevented them from devoting their full time to their pupils. Finally the Masters endeavoured to supplement their incomes by letting

---

[1] Samuel Story (Master, 1759-64), James Coery (Master, 1764-66), Samuel Reeve (Master, 1766-67), and John Franklin Squire (Master, Oct.-Dec. 1767.) In 1789 Reeve, when Senior Proctor, hung himself in Caius College. His body was not found for several months and the matter afforded scandal-mongers much speculation.

their house in Free School Lane.   Such few pupils as they had came to them in their college rooms. Even then the lessons given were infrequent and irregular, being scamped by masters and boys alike.

Fortunately, some of the Masters, who were appointed during this period of decline, did make slight efforts to avert impending ruin.   William White (Master, 1767-74), for instance, appears to have devoted a little attention to his scholars, for he has the credit of having produced one pupil who achieved a record in the annals of the Perse.   The boy in question was Robert Towerson Cory, who subsequently entered Emmanuel.[1]   After graduating as fifth wrangler, Cory became Fellow and subsequently Master of his college—the only Persean who has so filled such a post at either University.   From 1809 to 1813 he was also Knightbridge Professor of Moral Philosophy.

If the mere names of masters were a true indication of a school's prosperity, the Perse at this time should have been a flourishing school indeed.[2] White, for instance, had been Senior Wrangler ; Richard Fisher (afterwards Belward) became Master of Caius ; and John Jelliand Brundish obtained the

---

[1] Bowtell MSS. vii. 2724.

[2] The Masters at this period were William Bond (1774-75), Richard Fisher (1775-81), John Jelliand Brundish (1781-82), William Walford (Oct.-Dec. 1782), and Thomas Cooke Burroughes (1782-86).

THE SCHOOL HALL, CIRCA 1902

almost unique distinction of being Senior Wrangler, Senior Chancellor's Medallist, and Smith's Prizeman in one and the same year. The twelve months, however, during which the last-mentioned was Master of the Perse are a complete blank. Mr. Brundish received his stipend with the utmost regularity, but it is to be feared that he did nothing to earn it. By 1785, even the fiction of keeping the school open was abandoned. The Trustees still appointed masters, and the masters still received their stipends, but they had no pupils. It came to be almost the recognised custom for the Junior Fellows of Caius to hold the posts of Master and Usher in succession.

By this date the Master's house had fallen into far worse hands than the school itself. In or about 1780 it was occupied by Jemmy Gordon, a solicitor, who subsequently became a notorious character in Cambridge.

" At the expiration of his articles," as readers of Gunning's *Reminiscences* will recall, " he commenced to practise in Free School Lane, in the house which ought to have been occupied by the Master of the Perse School, but which was at that time (through the neglect of the Trustees) let to the highest bidder : here he led an expensive and profligate life, and placed at the head of his table a young woman of considerable beauty, who went by the soubriquet of the Duchess of Gordon. But Gordon's extravagance knew no bounds and he was compelled to go into cheaper and more obscure lodgings. He was then at the service of any man who thought proper to send him an invitation to entertain his friends and to get very drunk by way of recompense. Dressed in a huge cocked hat and the tarnished uniform of a general or admiral (for Jemmy was not too proud to accept any article of apparel that occasionally was given him from an old clothes shop) . . . this extraordinary character infested the streets swearing and blaspheming in a most horrible manner."

With the masters mere pensioners of Caius College, the scholars gone, and the school premises put to other and worse uses, it is not surprising to learn that the inhabitants of Cambridge were hardly aware of the existence of the benefaction of Stephen Perse. A strong and healthy public opinion would undoubtedly have made such ignorance impossible, and would not have tolerated such gross neglect of duty on the part of Masters and Trustees. Unfortunately, this was an age of municipal misgovernment and corruption, and in Cambridge, in particular, a proper sense of civic responsibility was entirely wanting. It almost appeared as if the Perse benefaction was destined to come to a dismal end. Fortunately, however, at an hour when the future prospects of the school seemed blackest, a single townsman started an agitation which saved the Perse from the oblivion threatening it. This agitator is known to us only by his pseudonym of

" An Inhabitant of Cambridge." He started his campaign in the *Cambridge Chronicle* on October 20th, 1787, when he made the following enquiries :

" I should esteem it a favour if some of your correspondents would inform me, whether our Free Grammar School has an endowment, and to what amount ? who is the Master, and by whom appointed ? whose children are entitled to admission at the School, and to whom should application be made for such admission ? "

In the following issue of the paper an answer is given, quoting from Carter's *History of Cambridge* and the Founder's will. But the matter did not rest here. An Inhabitant's enquiries appear to have caused the Trustees considerable uneasinesss, and it was probably they who inspired the reply which appeared in the *Chronicle* of November 17th following.

" If your correspondent who signs himself ' An Inhabitant of Cambridge ' in your paper of the 19th of October had applied to the Master or Fellows of Caius College, he would have received a satisfactory answer to all his queries respecting the Free School founded by Dr. Perse. Though I am not a member of that society, yet I can assure your readers, from the best authority, that the School was kept open as long as any boys were sent for education ; that the masters now are and always have been ready to admit scholars agreeable to the Will of the Founder ; and that the parents of children properly qualified have only themselves to blame if they do not reap the advantages of that beneficent foundation.

A GOWNSMAN."

" A Gownsman's " intrusion gave the matter the prominence it deserved, for it induced an old Persean to take up the cudgels on behalf of the parents, and he spoke out very plainly in a letter to the *Chronicle* a fortnight later. He undoubtedly gave the real cause for the closing of the Perse, and his genuine indignation at the treatment meted out to his old school may excuse faultiness in his English :

" Had your correspondent (who signs himself ' A Gownsman ') been as well acquainted as I am with the cause of the decline of the Free School, he would never have asserted that the parents of children were to blame for neglect, not the Masters of the School. I have only to observe, when Dr. Perse founded the Free School in Cambridge, it is clear he intended that the Master and his Assistants should attend the whole of the usual school hours ; but boys attending hours before the Master came, and when he did come staying so short a time, reduced the School to so small a number, that the Master totally gave up attendance at School, and ordered the boys to his room in college. If but one boy, should not the Masters being paid their salaries fulfil the will of the donor ?   ' The labourer is worthy of his hire.'   ONE EDUCATED IN THE SCHOOL."

From a note appended to this letter we learn that the agitation thus started by " An Inhabitant " bore good fruit. The governors authorised the printer of the *Chronicle* to inform his readers that the school would be re-opened immediately after the Christmas holidays.

CHAPTER VI

THE LAST DAYS OF THE ORIGINAL SCHEME
(1787-1841)

THE Master to whom was entrusted the task of setting the affairs of the Perse in order was the namesake and son of the Charles Davy who had been Usher between 1747 and 1751. The younger Davy had been appointed to his father's old post in 1785, and promoted to the Mastership a year later. For two years he had been content to follow the example of his predecessors and made no attempt to re-open the school. Nevertheless, when public opinion roused the Trustees to a proper sense of their responsibilities, he showed himself perfectly ready to carry out the duties attached to his post.

The same cannot be said of his Usher, Robert Forby, who resigned ten days after the first disturbing enquiries were made in the *Cambridge Chronicle*. Forby was famous in his day as a botanist and the philologist of the East Anglian dialect. He also made a reputation for himself as a private tutor.

Throughout his life he suffered from a slender purse and short temper. At a later period he once indulged in high words with the parent of one of his pupils, because that parent failed to understand that the obligation as between himself and his son's instructor " was perfectly mutual," and that tuition fees were not charitable doles. When Forby accepted a salaried post at the Perse School, there was created an obligation which was perfectly mutual. The acceptance of the salary without rendering any work in return made him the recipient of a charitable dole. Unfortunately for himself and for the school, Forby never realised this fact whilst he was Usher.

The difficulty of finding an Usher ready to undertake the actual duty of teaching was, it would seem, by no means easily solved. George Leonard Jenyns held the post and received the emoluments during the period between October and December, 1787. When the Trustees at length decided to re-open the school, he resigned. Fortunately, John Brinkley, his successor, proved more satisfactory. Brinkley was a distinguished mathematician, having only recently been Senior Wrangler and Smith's Prizeman. At the Perse he appears to have been conscientious in attending to his duties, but it was not to be expected that a man of his ability would be content to hold for long a poorly paid subordinate post in a small grammar school. In 1791 he left Cambridge to become Professor of Astronomy at Dublin University and Astronomer Royal of Ireland. In 1826, he was consecrated Bishop of Clogher.

When he re-opened the school, the younger Davy had one great advantage. He was in a position to strike out along new lines in education. His father's *Letters to a Young Gentleman*, published in 1787, might almost have been a teacher's manual specially designed for use at the Perse, the " Young Gentleman " being the new Master himself. As will be remembered, the *Letters* vigorously attacked the antiquated grammar school curriculum and advocated that greater attention should be paid in schools to the teaching of mathematics and science. The younger Davy was by inclination a scientist,[1] and his Usher was an able mathematician. Nothing, therefore, could have been more gratifying to the two Masters than to introduce the teaching of new subjects.

No reform, however, could be attended by any permanent success unless encouragement was received from the Trustees. Above all, financial

[1] Although in orders Davy took a degree in medicine. He took the living of Creeting, Suffolk, and died in 1836.

support was very necessary. Unfortunately, no support—financial or otherwise—was forthcoming. Nothing in fact better showed the entire lack of interest on the part of the Trustees than the action taken by them at the very time the school was re-opened. The revenue of the Perse Trust had by this date fully recovered, and was, in fact, more than doubled. Consequently it had become necessary to revise the apportionment of this income. The most equitable division which the Trustees could have made would, of course, have been to make a proportionate increase to each of the special objects of the Founder's benefaction. This course, however, was not adopted by the Trustees. They took full advantage of the clause in the Founder's will which empowered them to bestow any surplus income on such charitable objects as they in their discretion thought fit. The object which commended itself to their charity was their own college. The members of Caius College (including officers to whom Perse had left nothing in his will) were the only persons to benefit under the re-distribution. In spite of the fact that nearly one quarter of the original income of the Trust had been allotted to the school, not one penny was added to the stipends of the Master or Usher.

As they received no encouragement of any description, it is not surprising to learn that both Davy and Brinkley resigned at the end of three years. The school they left behind was poorly attended and insignificant. Nevertheless, the value of their work must not be gauged by the numbers or successes of their pupils. Had it not been for their care in these early days the school might once more have succumbed to neglect, for the Trustees' apathy was to continue for many years to come.

Davy's successor, John Drew Borton, held office for two years only and was succeeded by his Usher, John Spencer Cobbold (Master, 1793-94). This latter had graduated as a high wrangler, and had also been Norrisian Prizeman. During the twelve months he was at the Perse, he proved himself a capable teacher. One of his pupils showed sufficient ability to obtain a scholarship at Caius— the first Persean to proceed there for over one hundred years. Unfortunately, in the case of Cobbold the Perse suffered the fate which so often befalls a poorly endowed school. It served an able man as the stepping stone to further advancement. In 1794 he was appointed to the more lucrative headmastership of Nuneaton School, and left to take up his duties there.

After Cobbold's departure masters followed each

other in quick succession.[1]   The Trustees reverted to the old practice of appointing junior fellows of their college.   The inevitable result followed.   The school dwindled almost to vanishing point, and no more boys proceeded to the University.   In the greater world beyond Cambridge the Napoleonic wars were being waged.   As an indication of how inadequately the school was fulfilling its functions in national life, it must regretfully be placed on record that the Perse cannot claim as its own a single member of the British forces then in the field.[2]

In 1804 an improved rent roll once more enabled the Trustees to make a fresh distribution of the funds in their hands.   It is satisfactory to note that on this occasion the claims of the school were not wholly overlooked.   The Master's stipend was raised to £53 10s., and that of the Usher to £31 10s. Yet in view of the greatly increased cost of living this further remuneration was quite inadequate.   It was not as if the Trustees were unable to make a more

[1] The following were Masters of the Perse between 1794 and 1812 : St. John Smith (1794-95), Benedict Chapman (1795-99), George Grigby (1799-1802), William Gimingham (1802-04), William Wilkins (1804-05), Daniel Gwilt (1805-10), and John White (1810-12). They were all Fellows of Caius.

[2] George Grigby, who had been Master from 1799 to 1802, served in the First Dragoons and Eleventh Foot, rising to the rank of Captain.   He was drowned off Falmouth in 1811 when proceeding in a troopship to the Peninsula.

substantial increase, for the other beneficiaries under the Founder's will obtained proportionately far larger sums under this second redistribution. If the Trustees really expected the school's fortunes to revive after this additional grant, they were disappointed. Even with this increase in their salaries, the Masters did not receive a living wage. Consequently, it was impossible for them to devote their full time to the school. Writing in his *Cantabrigia Depicta* Harraden gives a melancholy account of the state of the school in 1809 :

" The school-house exists almost without scholars : the insufficiency of the salaries prevents a constant attendance of the masters, and therefore few boys attend—and those receive their lessons very frequently at their master's lodgings."

The *New Cambridge Guide* (published in the same year) provides further details and accounts for the decline of the Perse in very plain language :

" By some mismanagement the original intention of this excellent institution is perverted : as two or three scholars is generally the largest number at present educated, and these receive their lessons at the lodgings of the master. This abuse is the more to be regretted, as the children, generally speaking, of the poor inhabitants of Cambridge are rude and uninformed."

Three years after these words were penned, the Trustees came to the conclusion that the state of affairs described in these two books hardly reflected credit upon themselves. They saw that the curriculum provided was out of date, and empowered the Master to revise it. They also realised that fifty odd pounds was not an adequate salary for the Master and raised it to £120. To provide money for this increased stipend they abolished the post of Usher. At the same time they reduced the number of places on the foundation to sixteen—a reduction which inflicted hardship on nobody, if three was generally the largest number of boys attending the school. The governors also empowered the headmaster to take non-foundationers into the school and charge an entrance fee of one guinea, and also a guinea a quarter for instructing them, " to say nothing," in the words of a hostile critic of these changes, " of a miserable exaction of 2s. 6d. per annum for candle and firing." As earnest of their changed attitude towards the school, they took advantage of the resignation of John White, then Master, to break away from the harmful tradition of the past, and appoint a man who was not a member of Caius. Their choice fell on John Wilson, formerly chaplain of Trinity. They insisted on his residing in the school premises, and assigned both masters' houses to him.

The townspeople of Cambridge received a printed

circular informing them of these changes, and the resulting benefits which it was hoped the school would derive therefrom. Unfortunately—but at the same time perhaps inevitably—the inhabitants of Cambridge received the information with marked coldness. To them the chief recommendation of the Perse had been the gratuitous education which it provided for an almost unlimited number of boys. If payment was now to be demanded they could point to several private schools in and near Cambridge which could provide a much better education at the same cost. Furthermore, they saw that in the absence of an Usher, the Master would be hampered if he had to manage many more boys than sixteen. Local hostility was so pronounced that the scheme appeared to be almost foredoomed to complete failure. Very shortly afterwards the Trustees wisely rescinded the most obnoxious of all the new regulations—that empowering the Master to charge non-foundationers.

It would have required a man of considerable character to surmount the difficulties which impeded the growth of the school. Unfortunately Wilson's talents were distinctly mediocre. During the thirteen years in which he was Master, only one boy is known to have proceeded from the Perse to the University. The number of boys attending the school remained practically stationary at sixteen. The Trustees themselves were keenly disappointed with the results achieved by their reforms. What with the cold water poured by the townspeople on their well-meant scheme and the inefficiency of the Master, it seemed hopeless to restore the bygone prestige of the Perse. Instead of setting to work to try to popularise the new scheme or to find a more satisfactory Master, the governors once more became apathetic. At the time the Trust enjoyed a very large surplus income, which might well have been devoted to the improvement of the school. Such an idea never suggested itself to the governors. Strewed up and down the accounts we find such items as, " A sufferer by fire at Chesterton, £1," and " to Mrs. Wilson's sister, £2 "—excellent objects of charity, no doubt, but not those which the Founder intended to benefit. Certainly the ten pounds bestowed in 1817 as a " Donation to Charity Schools," could have been more profitably and properly spent nearer home.

As the number of boys attending the Perse never reached a score, the very limited premises in Free School Lane were more than adequate for Wilson's requirements. In 1816 this fact came to the notice of the University, which, at the beginning of that year, had under the will of Viscount Fitzwilliam received a handsome bequest of pictures as well as a sum of £100,000 to build a museum to house the collection. Until the museum could be built the pictures required a resting place, and a syndicate was appointed to consider the question of temporary accommodation. On April 27th, 1816, three members of this syndicate came to inspect the school buildings. They were received by Wilson, who showed them over the premises, including the schoolroom. He informed the gentlemen that he did " not make much use of this room except during the hot weather." Having made a careful inspection the members of the syndicate came to the conclusion that after certain structural alterations had been made, the room would be well adapted for housing the Fitzwilliam collection. The Trustees made no difficulty about acceding to their application, and even agreed to allow the University the use of the northern wing of the buildings when they asked for it. All they stipulated was that the syndics should provide at their own expense a new room and offices for the Master, and should also bear the cost of restoring the building to its former state on the expiration of their tenancy. Accordingly by the end of June, 1816, Master and boys migrated from the schoolhouse to the premises in the south wing. The school was destined never to

P.S.   G

return to its original home.   When the Fitzwilliam syndicate surrendered the premises in 1842, the building was pulled down and a new one erected in its place.

A contemporary print shows the interior of the old school as it was when it housed the Fitzwilliam collection.   As this is the only view of the interior we have, and as the Fitzwilliam syndics made considerable structural alterations, a few words of description will not be out of place.   The room as depicted is serving the twofold purpose of a picture gallery and a museum.   The original windows were concealed behind the wainscot bookcases lining the walls, and in their place skylights were contrived in the open roof.   The room itself was lengthened by the syndics by taking in a portion of the Usher's house on the north side.   To obtain a better effect the syndics removed the upper floor and partitions of this portion of the buildings.   The architect responsible for these alterations was William Wilkins, who had been Master from 1804 to 1806— an absolutely blank period in the school's history. In 1816 he was called upon to complete the wreck of that which, with a little effort, he might ten years before have piloted to safety.

There is nothing to record of the last nine years of Wilson's rule.   The school remained in exile and obscurity until his resignation in 1825. Although this first experiment of appointing a Master from another college than Caius failed, the Trustees fortunately did not consider that failure afforded an excuse for reverting to their old custom. As in 1812, they went to Trinity for their Master. On this occasion their choice fell on James Bailey. Their new Master was one of the most brilliant of all the classical scholars who have had charge of the Perse. In his undergraduate days Bailey won the Browne Medals for Greek Ode and Greek Epigram, as well as the Members' Latin Essay Prize. His work at that period brought him to the notice of Sir Walter Scott, who not only endeavoured to obtain a librarianship in Edinburgh for him, but also gave the struggling student financial assistance.[1] Throughout his life, Bailey was a frequent writer for the *Classical Journal*. Perhaps his best known contribution to classical study is his edition of Facciolati's *Latin Dictionary*, which he published whilst he was at the Perse. Another work produced by him during this period of headmastership was an annotated edition of Dalzel's *Analecta Graeca Minora*. He was, moreover, something more than a scholar. He could inspire in others a warm

---

[1] Letters from Scott to Bailey are now to be seen in the Fitzwilliam Museum.

enthusiasm for his favourite studies. His pupils always spoke of him with affection and esteem. Into many he inculcated a deep love of classical learning and a true spirit of poetry. Some of his boys did their Master infinite credit in later life. Considering the smallness of the school the number of boys he sent to the University was quite remarkable, five of them becoming Fellows of their respective colleges.

One of the first steps taken by Bailey was to remove the impression that the school was intended exclusively for the benefit of the sixteen foundationers. For this purpose he caused a notice to be circulated to the following effect :

" The stipends specified in the will of Dr. Perse appearing to the Trustees to be an inadequate remuneration for the education of one hundred scholars, it has been agreed by them to reduce the number of *free* scholars to sixteen. The School has of late been considerably improved : it having been deemed advisable by the present headmaster, that, exclusively of a knowledge of the Greek and Latin languages, and of Greek, Latin, and English composition (for which only the original institution provided), the scholars should likewise be instructed in the ordinary branches of education, together with the elements of mathematics."

Though, not unnaturally, there was considerable feeling locally over the continued reduction in the number of free places, the prospect of obtaining a sound education along modern lines restored confidence in the Perse. Bailey's undoubted ability proved that this confidence was not mistaken, and the numbers attending the school rose rapidly. From sixteen they quickly mounted to thirty: before Bailey left they were over fifty. The distinctions gained by many of his pupils mark Bailey's Mastership as one of the most successful epochs in the history of the school. The class list for midsummer 1837 is interesting reading. There were twelve boys in the top class, and of these no less than eight proceeded to the University, seven graduating in honours.

In addition to day boys, the headmaster took in a few boarders from outside Cambridge. In 1827 he had to obtain assistance. He called in a member of his own college, Francis Reveley. The Trustees' account books contain no record of the payment of a regular stipend to Reveley or to any other assistant. Bailey must therefore have provided the Usher's salary out of his own pocket. Unfortunately, this outgoing tended rather to hamper the school's progress. Although he was treated by the Trustees with far greater liberality than Wilson, Bailey was never free from financial embarrassment. Constant illness and general inability to understand monetary matters kept him in continual straits. Although his salary rose gradually from £125 to £450, he was frequently in debt, and on one occasion had to obtain a loan from the Trustees, which he never succeeded in repaying. In the end he was obliged to compound with his creditors. His financial troubles were, however, by no means so dire as those of Reveley. The unfortunate Usher had to subsist on the pittance Bailey could afford to pay him. He, too, got into debt, and his creditors were far more insistent in their demands. He had the debtor's jail constantly before his eyes, and on one occasion only escaped incarceration through the timely intervention of the Master of Caius.

Some interesting reminiscences of the Perse as it was in the thirties were recorded in the school magazine of April, 1905. They are those of the late Mr. D. V. Mordecai, who was at the school from 1834 to 1840.

" Mr. Mordecai was a Foundation Scholar, as indeed were all the boys. The way in which he was elected compares curiously with the present system. Being then about nine years old, he went with his father to see Mr. Bailey (then Headmaster) at his house next the School, and was told to read a chapter in the Bible. After reading about half-a-dozen verses, Mr. Bailey said, ' That's quite sufficient, I'll pass you,' and his father was forthwith instructed to get him a Latin Grammar of Mr. Hall (the grandfather of the present bookseller). His formal appointment as scholar was made by Dr. Davy (then Master of Caius College, in whose hands the government of the School was at that time), and it was Mr. Turnbull, a Fellow of Caius, who gave him his recommendation. The Foundation Scholarship carried with it the right to free rooms and lectures, if the boy reached the top of the School and entered Caius College, and the estimated cost of the College education was not more than £90 for the three years. . . .

" After mastering a certain amount of Latin Grammar, learning much of it by heart, Mr. Mordecai went on to the *Electa*, a book of short Latin pieces. Then came the *Delectus*, Eutropius, Cornelius Nepos and Ovid in the order named. At this point he began Greek, having then learned little but the alphabet. When he had done some Elementary Grammar, he started the Gospel of S. John in Greek. The next classical author was Virgil, and at this point the Classical studies of those who were not going to the first class stopped. There were six classes (Class I. being the head), and Mr. Mordecai was top of the second class when he left. Boys were allowed one month after leaving, during which they might return to the School if they or their parents altered their minds. Mr. Mordecai's month was extended to two, because (as we may safely conjecture) they were unwilling to lose so promising a pupil.

" In Mathematics the boys were taught Arithmetic, Algebra, Euclid, Trigonometry, and Conic Sections. They learnt practically no English Grammar, and very little Geography. One afternoon in each week was devoted to English History and one to Roman History. Once a week they read from the Bible and learnt the Creed, the Ten Commandments, and so on, and sometimes read (say) some of the poems of Cowper or Cottle (for further information as to whom I refer my readers to the *Dictionary of National Biography*). For home work they never had more than twenty lines of (say) Ovid or Virgil, and about half-a-dozen verses in the Greek Testament.

" The School hours were from 9 to 12 and 2 to 4, with half-holidays on Wednesdays and Saturdays and a whole day's holiday on the more important Church Festivals. For holidays they had a fortnight at Easter, five weeks at Midsummer, a fortnight at Stourbridge Fair time and five weeks at Christmas.

" The masters did not wear gowns during school hours. The boys sat at long desks, which were furnished with inkwells, and lockers covered by flaps."

Bailey appears to have taken charge of part of the mathematical as well as the classical teaching. He did not find himself interfered with by intruding governors, but was left to manage the school very much as he liked. The first governor to take any active interest in the school was Dr. Benedict Chapman, who had been Master from 1796 to 1799. Shortly after his election to the Mastership of Caius in 1839, Chapman paid a visit to the school. Mr. Mordecai remembered

" his going round the School in his black knee breeches and gaiters, and Mr. Barber's suggesting that a bolt should be put on the gate and that a boy should be appointed to lock it at 9 o'clock in order that the evil habits of the unpunctual might be more patently advertised. Mr. Barber suggested Mr. Mordecai, and Dr. Chapman appointed him."

Even to the schoolboy mind this reform would appear but trivial. But what was it that brought so important a personage as the Master of Caius to see the school, whose existence so many of his predecessors had ignored ? His presence was due to an agitation for reforms of far greater magnitude—reforms which when achieved were to confer great benefits on the Perse. But the events leading up to and resulting from this agitation require a whole chapter to themselves.

CHAPTER VII

FROM ONE REFORM MOVEMENT TO ANOTHER
(1833-73)

It must not be supposed that during all the years of neglect the word " reform " was never mentioned in connection with the Perse Trust. Other objects of the Founder's benefaction had suffered in the same manner as the school. Whereas the Master and four senior Fellows of Caius had between 1812 and 1830 raised their own stipends from the original £9 per annum ordained by the Founder to £840 per annum, the Perse Fellows at the same college had still to subsist on the pittances given to them under the Founder's will. This, however, could not go long without comment. In 1830 two of the Perse Fellows, H. O. Martin and Daniel Maude, made a strong remonstrance against the prevailing practice and demanded that the Perse scholars and Fellows should also receive an augmentation of their salaries. This remonstrance led to an examination into the history and administration of the trust.

In consequence of the resulting disclosures, Henry Bickersteth (better known at a later date as Lord Langdale and Master of the Rolls), who was then one of the four senior Fellows, " felt so convinced that he had improperly (but unwittingly, for he did not reside here) received sums intended for other uses, that he voluntarily refunded a sum of nearly £800, and he then, or soon afterwards, gave up his fellowship." An interesting commentary to this very honourable action of Mr. Bickersteth is to be found in the conduct of the recipients of this £800. " The sum returned," we are told, " was carried regularly to account merely as ' Received of Mr. Bickersteth ' ! ! ! ! and though, in consequence of the increase in the stipends of the Perse Fellows, the Master and four Seniors were obliged to reduce their salaries in the course of that year, yet no other effect seems to have been produced by Mr. Bickersteth's honourable and manly conduct."

Beyond the precincts of Caius there was an increasing feeling of dissatisfaction as to the way in which the Trust was being administered. As has been seen, the voice of dissatisfaction was first heard amongst the townspeople in 1812, when it was suggested to impose a quarterly tuition fee. But in those days, with a corrupt and inefficient Corporation governing the borough, there was no organisation in the town which could reasonably hope to conduct a successful agitation for reformation in the management of the Perse School. By 1833, however, all this was changed. The old municipal Corporation was on its last legs, and reform in every walk of civic life was the political battle-cry of the hour. By now the agitators for reform in the school were an organised body, and spoke with no uncertain voice.

The reform party seem to have made representations to the governors, and to have requested them to draw up a plan for a more equitable distribution of the trust funds, the appointment of a regular Usher, and the increase in the number of free places to one hundred. Apparently the reply received did not give satisfaction. A public meeting was called to protest against the manner in which the school was being managed. As a result of this meeting, it was decided to proceed by way of information against the Trustees. Accordingly, in 1833, an information was filed against them at the relation of Jeremiah Thring, William Reeves, and William Metcalfe. The relators prayed for an account of the property applicable for the purposes of the charity as declared in the Wills of the Founder and Griffith, and more particularly for an account of that property applicable for the purposes of the school.

After asking for a declaration that the rents of the Free School Lane property belonged exclusively to the school, the relators went on to demand that the Master and four senior Fellows and Bailey (who was also made a defendant) should be made personally answerable for any part of the income which the Court should find to have been misapplied by them. In particular, it was asked that the Master of Caius (Dr. Davy) and Dr. Woodhouse (the senior Fellow),[1] should be ordered to refund all the monies they had wrongly received under the various schemes of redistribution since 1804. Finally, the relators prayed that the Master and four senior Fellows might be deprived of all control of the school.

Soon after the proceedings were instituted a pamphlet was printed, which gives much interesting information as to the evidence upon which the relators relied. The pamphlet takes the form of an open letter from a pseudonymous Lancelot Probe to a pseudonymous Gamaliel Thorn. It is rather surprising to find statements of this character appearing in print at a time when the suit was still pending, but it is still more surprising to learn of the methods employed to obtain the evidence for which the writer sought :

[1] He was Usher of the Perse from 1806 to 1812.

" My dear Thorn," writes Probe, " I no sooner received your note respecting Perse's Free School, than I sent for our worthy little friend Simpkins, and by his interference I succeeded, though with some difficulty, in procuring the loan for a short time of the papers, from which I have extracted the following information ; upon the accuracy of which, I assure you his lordship [sc. the judge] may implicitly rely."

Comment is almost superfluous. It was only a most extraordinary method of eliciting information from an opponent in a lawsuit.

Howbeit, at this date we have no need to discuss the ethics of the transaction. What we have to consider is the evidence, which Probe, with the co-operation of Simpkins, was able to obtain. They certainly made a very exhaustive search of the documents they were thus able to borrow, and some of the facts published to the world in the open letter are of very material interest. Some of these facts have already been referred to in this book, but for the purpose of making clear the exact manner in which the trust funds had been dealt with, I think it will not be amiss to repeat them here and to add certain additional facts, which Lancelot Probe brought to light.

The bulk of the letter deals with the application of the income of the Trust. Probe points out that this income had risen from £250 per annum at the time of Perse's death to roughly £2000 per annum in 1829.

" You are of course aware," he goes on to say, " that on general principles the objects of the charitable trusts ought to receive any benefit which may arise from the increase, or suffer any loss from the decrease, of the trust *proportionably*. In order to show how proportion has been violated in this case, I beg your attention to the following account of the expenditure for the year 1829, which it will be curious to compare with the statement before given from Dr. Perse's will."

For clearness and convenience' sake the two statements referred to are subjoined in tabular form :

	UNDER THE FOUNDER'S WILL.				IN 1829.				
	£	s.	d.	£ s. d.	£	s.	d.	£ s. d.
Free School								
Master - -	40	0	0		150	0	0	
Usher - -	20	0	0	60 0 0	0	0	0	150 0 0
Almshouses - -				24 0 0				120 0 0
Caius College—								
Master - -	3	0	0		280	0	0	
Four Senior Fellows -	6	0	0		560	0	0	
Perse and Frankland Fellows }	78	0	0		390	0	0	
Perse Scholars -	24	0	0		144	0	0	
College Chest and other College Officers - -	17	11	4	128 11 4	298	0	0	1672 0 0
Town of Cambridge New River and Barnwell Causeway - - }				18 0 0				0 0 0
Anniversary -				5 3 4				16 0 9
Poor of Massingham, Marpley, and Barley }				6 0 0				6 0 0
			Total	243 14 8			Total	1967 0 9

From the above statistics Probe made the following deductions :

"Taking the increase to be one-eighth of the original endowment, the following will be a statement of the profit and loss of a few of the principal objects of the charity in the year referred to (in other words, the sums which some were overpaid and the others underpaid).

PROFIT.				LOSS.			
	£	s.	d.		£	s.	d.
Master of Caius Coll.	256	o	o	Free School - -	330	o	o
Four senior Fellows -	512	o	o	Perse and Frankland			
College Chest, etc. -	91	9	4	Fellows - -	230	o	o
	859	9	4		560	o	o

"The coolness with which the Master and four seniors (themselves the trustees) raised their own stipends from £9 to £840 per annum, must excite in the breasts of the old Corporators [sc. of Cambridge] a conscious sense of their inferiority in the practice of that charity which begins at home. . . .

"Dr. Perse in his will gave nothing whatever to the Deans, the Steward, the Conduct, the College Registrar, or the Gardener ; but his faithful trustees have no scruple in extending to these meritorious personages the benefit of his munificence, and in 1799 the sum of £800 was paid out of the trust fund towards the sum expended by the college in repairs and new buildings, and in a contribution to government *for the internal defence* of the country ! ! ! "

The most serious of all Probe's allegations are those made with reference to the manner in which the accounts were kept. They are repeated here for what they are worth, although without impeaching his veracity a search in the trust account books has not confirmed the first charge brought against the bursar. After referring to the Founder's directions as to the auditing of the accounts, the letter goes on to say that these audits have

" never been done within memory, and the accounts (kept infinitely worse than churchwardens' or constables' accounts are usually kept in country villages), are audited by the Trustees themselves :—with what *care* will appear from these facts. In one year the Bursar made a mistake (*of course in his own favour*) of £100 in adding up the account, and this mistake, palpable as it is, has never yet been rectified, and in more modern times a mistake of more than £100 in *the Bursar's favour* was not discovered until the second audit afterwards. On another occasion, a tax of about £25 was suffered to creep into the account, although it was imposed on property with which the Trust had nothing whatever to do."

Reverting to the school itself Probe complains of the reduction of the number of the free scholars, the abolition of the post of Usher, the handing over of the school premises to the Fitzwilliam Museum, and the imposition of school fees.[1]

Although this open letter did not constitute the

[1] The pamphlet from which the above statements are taken is entitled *A Letter to the Burgesses of Cambridge on the approaching municipal elections. By Gamaliel Thorn, Esq. With an appendix relative to the Perse Free School, Cambridge* : printed at Cambridge, 1835.

pleadings of the relators,[1] it gives in greater detail the substance of their charges. The defendants' pleadings have not been traced by me, but they appear to have consisted in a more or less categorical denial of the charges brought against them, and a strong rebuttal of the imputation of bad faith in their dealings with the trust funds.

The law is proverbially slow, and the case in question proved no exception to the rule. The defendants petitioned to have the action dismissed as vexatious, but failed in their attempt. Finally, the action came on for trial in the Rolls Court in April, 1837. It is interesting to note that the presiding judge was Henry Bickersteth, then Lord Langdale. The hearing before him occupied three days. No very determined defence was offered. The Master and Fellows at the Bar admitted that there had been irregularities in the administration of the trust funds. In extenuation they pleaded that their attention had never been seriously drawn to the subject until about 1830, and that then they had done their best to remedy past errors. They now were prepared to offer every facility for reorganising the trust. As a defence against the

[1] The pleadings in this case have not yet been discovered. They have been wrongly filed at the Record Office. It is to be hoped that some subsequent historian of the School will be more successful in his search for them.

charge of misapplication of the trust funds they relied on their own particular interpretation of the clause in Perse's will directing the surplus income of the charity to be " from time to time bestowed as my Executors for their times, and after my Supervisors, shall think fit."

Lord Langdale delivered judgment on July 31st, 1837. He pointed out that the difficulty as to the true construction of the Founder's will arose from the fact that Perse conceived of his charity only as receiving a permanently fixed annual income, whereas that income had proved to be a very varying sum of money. With regard to the clause dealing with surplus income, he held that no beneficial gift was thereby made to Caius College, but that the clause was a specific direction to bestow such money upon charitable uses. Lord Langdale went on to declare that the principal object of Dr. Perse's benefaction was without doubt the school, and that it was clearly to the school that the greater portion of the trust income should be devoted. He had been asked to remove the Master and Fellows of Caius from their trusteeship : that, he felt, he could not possibly do. " When I see how anxiously the Founder in this case had connected his foundation with the college and the utter impossibility of separating the one from the other without defeating his plain and manifest intention, I conceive it to be perfectly clear that the college cannot be removed from the office of trustees." Neither could he see his way to order the Master and Dr. Woodhouse to refund the moneys they had received, as they had participated in the division of the trust moneys with persons, who were equally culpable, but who were then dead, and therefore not before the Court.

Lord Langdale further declared that the sum of £100 was subject to the trusts of the will of George Griffith, and that the school buildings and the adjoining house in Free School Lane belonged exclusively to the school. He referred it to a Master in Chancery to approve of a scheme for the general administration of the property and to settle a scheme for the future conduct and management of the school. In settling such scheme the Master was to be at liberty to approve of a plan for adding instruction in writing and arithmetic to the curriculum prescribed by the Founder.

Another four years passed before the new proposals for administering the trust received judicial sanction. On July 31st, 1841, Sir Giffin Wilson, the Master to whom the cause had been referred, gave his approval to a revised scheme. In the first place, the Master assented to a proposal for rebuilding the school premises, and directed that a sum of

£2600 should be set aside out of the trust funds for that purpose. The minimum salary attached to the headmastership was fixed at £300, and that attached to the post of Usher at £150.

The rules prescribed for the conduct and management of the school kept as nearly as possible both to the letter and the spirit of the Founder's will and the ordinances made by his Executors in 1621. It is pleasing to see the old regulation which ordered a decent oaken board to be hung up in the school with the scholars' names inscribed thereon, repeated word for word. The Usher was still required to keep a register of admissions, and produce it to the Perse Registrar for transcription. Preference was still to be accorded to boys educated at the school in appointment to scholarships and fellowships on the Perse foundation at Caius, and to the posts of Master and Usher of the school.

Here and there, however, alterations had to be made to adapt the school to modern requirements. The number of free scholars remained at one hundred—to be drawn from Cambridge and the three adjacent villages, but the new rules went into more detail with regard to the mode of choosing them. Elections to vacancies were to be held four times a year. The Perse Registrar was to give at least seven days' warning of the meetings to be held to make such elections, by inserting a notice to that effect in one or more of the local newspapers and by posting a similar notice outside the school door. Scholars were to be between ten and fourteen years old at the time of their election, and were not to remain longer than the midsummer vacation after they should attain the age of eighteen. Morning school was to begin at nine and last till twelve; afternoon school was to begin at two and last till five. The new scheme also ordained early morning school in summer time, which was to begin at seven and last for an hour, but this rule very speedily fell into abeyance. Saturday was to be a half-holiday, and the Master was empowered to grant at his discretion eight whole holidays and twelve other half-holidays during the year. December 14th, being the day now fixed for celebrating the Founder's obit, was to be a whole holiday.

The Master was permitted to take in paying scholars provided he took " such further sufficient help " besides his regular staff as the Trustees should think fit. These non-foundationers paid an entrance fee of £5 and a half-yearly fee of £1, which fees were to be divided between the headmaster and Usher. To provide for an additional master, who was to be called the Assistant Usher, the governors were empowered to charge free scholars an entrance

THE PERSE PLAYERS IN 'THE DEATH OF ROLAND,' 1921

fee of thirty shillings and a half-yearly fee of ten shillings.

The vacations were to be five weeks at Christmas commencing on December 19th, ten days at Easter commencing the day before Good Friday, and five weeks at Midsummer commencing on June 18th. Within one week of the Midsummer holidays the free scholars were to be examined " as to their proficiency in classical and mathematical learning " by two persons of the standing of M.A., appointed by the Trustees. The examiners were to class the boys according to merit and award prizes on the examination.

Before dealing with the history of the school under this new scheme, it will be necessary to go back a few years and give an account of the events happening in the school whilst the suit in Chancery was pending. After the information was filed, the Trustees endeavoured to set the school's affairs in better order. In 1833 they appointed a regular Usher and made him an allowance in lieu of a house, his proper residence being still in the hands of the Fitzwilliam syndics. At Lady Day in the same year Bailey resigned. His health had not been good for some time past, and he had been absent from school most of the previous autumn. He appears to have been worried amongst other things by the

Chancery suit, in which it will be remembered he was a defendant, and his medical advisers strongly recommended him to give up his work. The Trustees recognised his services to the school in a very generous manner by granting him a pension. It is gratifying to note that the Court of Chancery subsequently confirmed this grant, and at the same time refused to make any order as to costs against Bailey. The work he did for the Perse merited better treatment than proceedings in Chancery, and it was well that he was compensated for the worries and anxieties of the lawsuit by appreciation in such a tangible form. Bailey left Cambridge for London, where he appears to have supplemented his pension by writing for the Classical and other journals, but his latter days were not entirely free from financial trouble. However, a Civil List Pension, awarded in recognition of his services to classical study, helped to alleviate the anxieties of his declining years.

The governors did not at once appoint a successor to Bailey. They placed a newly elected Fellow of Caius in temporary charge of the school. This was Charles Clayton, who had formerly been one of Bailey's most successful pupils. Whilst at the University he was a Browne's Medallist on two occasions. Later in life he became well known as a popular college tutor, but perhaps he is best remembered in Cambridge as vicar of Holy Trinity, where he proved an able successor to Charles Simeon. He had charge of the Perse for a single year only, but subsequently as an examiner and a member of the governing body he took a warm interest in his old school. Not a few Perseans owed much of their success in after life to the kindly advice and encouragement he offered them whilst they were still schoolboys.

In April, 1837, the governors chose Peter Mason of St. John's College as headmaster. He was a distinguished mathematician, having graduated third wrangler in the year in which Sir George Airy was senior. To Mason was entrusted the task of carrying the revised scheme into effect. For the first five years he taught in the southern wing of the school buildings, where Bailey had taught before him. In 1842 the Fitzwilliam collection was moved out of the schoolhouse proper, and in pursuance of the order of the Court the whole of the buildings were rebuilt and enlarged. Mason and his Usher, the Rev. George Barber, were driven out of their houses for the time being, but the governors made them an allowance in lieu of residence. By 1844 a new range of buildings was ready for the reception of Masters and boys. The architect, Mr. John Smith, retained the old quadrangle formation of the original buildings, and the old schoolroom with its fine Jacobean roof was preserved almost intact. The lighting of this room was improved by the insertion of large three-light windows with diamond shaped panes.   An honours board was hung up on one of the walls of the room, but it was chiefly remarkable for its lacunæ, for Jeremy Taylor's successes were immediately followed by those of the late locum tenens, Charles Clayton.   Another embellishment was " a splendid globe three feet in diameter, and weighing three stone, suspended for convenience from the roof," which evoked the admiration of a contemporary guidebook.   The two masters' houses, lying on either side of the school-room, were rebuilt on a more commodious scale.

The number of pupils had to be strictly limited until these buildings were ready for the full hundred boys.   At the end of 1844 Mason had hardly as many as twenty boys to teach, but as soon as the new premises were opened the numbers rose instantaneously to one hundred.   At the same time an Assistant Usher, the Rev. E. W. Gilbert, appeared on the scene.   The school was divided into six classes, of which the first was the highest.   Every boy was placed in the sixth or lowest class on joining the school.   The Master took this class and the first, and was thus able to make the acquaintance and gauge the calibre of each newcomer. Mr. Barber took the second and third classes, and Mr. Gilbert the fourth and fifth. Greek, Latin, and Arithmetic were the subjects taught in the lower classes. Homer, Xenophon, Anacreon and Virgil were read in the first class : the second learnt Ovid and the Greek Testament : in the fourth the boys used the Eton Grammar, Valpy's *Syntax and Prosody* and a book entitled *Propria quæ maribus*. None of the Masters were classical scholars and so the education in this subject was not so efficient as perhaps it ought to have been. At this period the Perse might almost be called an exclusively mathematical school. Not only did classics fall far behind the standard attained in many other schools of the same size, but general English subjects were almost totally neglected. The second class was supposed to read Goldsmith's Geography, but a scholar of this period informs us :

" Of English the utmost search of calls of memory reveals only some Geography with Mr. Gilbert in some lower class, and some Shakespeare read round boy by boy without pause for comment or explanation in the first form. Of modern languages or science, music or drawing, there was nothing whatever in connection with the school."

The books in use for religious instruction were Watts' *Scripture History* and Pinnock's *Catechism*.

Peter Mason was more fortunate than his predecessors in that he succeeded in interesting several members of the governing body in the school. Amongst these the name of Charles Clayton has already been mentioned. Another was the future Sir George Paget, who was appointed Perse Registrar in 1836. He started a school admission register which is still to be seen in the Caius College Treasury, many of its pages being written in his beautifully clear handwriting. He was also in the habit of being present at the Midsummer examinations, and in many other ways showing an interest in the boys. It is with no surprise, therefore, that we read of a whole holiday being given on December 12, 1851, "on account of Dr. Paget's Marriage yesterday." The connection of his family with the school did not end then. Some half a century later a grandson of Sir George Paget entered the Perse, and to-day his name can be seen inscribed on one of the Honours Shields and Fellowship Board adorning the School Hall.

The Master has left behind an interesting record of the holidays given by him. General Fasts and Days of Humiliation during the Crimean War and Indian Mutiny are whole holidays. The capture of Sebastopol and the signing of the Peace in 1856 are events to be celebrated by a whole day off school.

Equally interesting are the holidays given on December 4, 1857, " in order to give us an opportunity of hearing Dr. Livingstone," and on March 15, 1858, " to enable the boys and masters to see the great eclipse of the sun." But the headmaster must have felt proudest of all on April 4, 1854, when there was " a Whole Holiday By order of the Trustees, P. H. Mason, late a student of this school [and his own son] being elected a Fellow of St. John's College." The son's success was but one of many. Four other pupils of Mason obtained fellowships at different colleges. Their success was in a very large measure due to the headmaster's inspiration.

" Every boy felt and knew," says one of his pupils, " that as soon as he developed the slightest spark of Mathematical taste he found in his head master a firm friend, a teacher, and more, a worker with him, absolutely untiring in his efforts to clear away difficulties and encourage him to make big his aims."

One of Mason's pupils stands out pre-eminently above all his schoolfellows, not only as a great scholar, but as a great patriot. Edward Henry Palmer, an orphan, was admitted at Lady Day, 1851, being then just ten years old. Few biographies are more interesting than that of Palmer, written by his friend, Walter Besant, but a few fresh facts concerning Palmer's school days have come to light since Besant wrote his book, and they will be of interest to all Perseans who are proud of their departed worthies. Palmer was three years at the Perse, and then left on account of ill health. But in that brief period he revealed some of that talent which afterwards brought him into such prominence. He was little over fourteen when he left, and it was still, in Besant's words, " the days of small beginnings." Placed at first like any other new-comer in the bottom class, he quickly worked his way up to the top but one, where he arrived before he was thirteen. At the end of his first year his name appeared in the prize list as the winner of a divinity prize open to the whole school. Had his constitution been more robust at this period in his life, he would probably have won a scholarship at the University, and thus have been spared those years of struggle which preceded his admission to St. John's. He left when he was too young to have attracted the attention of his masters.

" He was not," says Besant, " a bookworm, nor was he precocious. . . . He always disliked mathematics. . . . Those who remember him at that time, and were his schoolfellows, say that he was always small, and apparently weak of frame, yet that he could do things which proved great muscular strength and endurance ; thus he was admirable on the trapeze and gymnastic bars, and he was a bold and fearless swimmer. He took no part in the cricket field or at football, but he was clever with his fingers and he was constantly making or devising things ; he read a great deal, especially poetry; and he was greatly caressed and petted by everybody, partly on account of a general belief that he would die early, partly on account of the singular personal charm which was always his most striking characteristic.

" He began to feel his way in languages while still a boy at school, independently of his Latin and Greek. He learned Romany. This is not a language with a grammar, save at those heights of pure Romany to which few of the People attain. It is a vocabulary. The boy learned it by paying travelling tinkers sixpence for a lesson, by haunting the tents, talking to the men, and crossing the women's palms with his pocket money in exchange for a few more words to add to his vocabulary. In this way he gradually made for himself a gipsy dictionary. No one of all those who have been attracted by these picturesque wanderers knew them better, or could more readily enter into their minds than Palmer—not even his brother in Romany lore, Charles Leland. This acquisition of Romany is the only achievement of his school days in which one can find promise of the later days. There are not, it may be owned, many schoolboys who save up their pocket-money in order to take lessons of tramps and vagabonds in the gipsy tongue."

The rest of his life—his distinguished University career, his great ride through the desert to his death amongst the Arabs, and his honoured grave in St. Paul's—belongs to the whole English nation, and the story has been told by Besant in a biography in words which every Persean of spirit will be the better for reading.

Besant is probably right in suggesting that the Perse did not give Palmer everything which a school ought to give. It is to be feared that the Perse in his days was altogether lacking in any sort or form of school life or patriotism outside the school walls. As a contemporary says :

" There was no organization of games, no school eleven, no school anything. Once outside the door of that big school the units fell to pieces for want of social cement, each going his own way to his house or to companions of his own choosing, doing exactly what was right in his own eyes. A shy self-conscious boy gained nothing but intellectual advantages—only part of what a school can give."

To this lack of a proper *esprit de corps* must in a large measure be attributed the woeful decline in the discipline of the school in the sixties. So long as Mason was young and active, and so long as he could depend on the loyal assistance of his colleagues, discipline was good. But the day came when the Master grew past his work, and as often as not illness prevented him from coming to the school. Unfortunately, one of his assistants, a fiery Irishman, proved not only incapable of maintaining order but also openly disloyal to his chief. This Irishman succeeded Mr. Barber as Usher in 1861, and was soon afterwards left virtually in charge of the school. Under him the lack of discipline became so appalling that several prominent inhabitants of Cambridge made a public protest to the Trustees.

The reply did not prove conciliatory, and the memorialists then enlisted the sympathy of the Town Council, which appointed a committee to enquire into the alleged defects of the school and to consider the most satisfactory means of placing the Perse more under popular control. Unfortunately this committee made very little progress. Its efforts were hampered by the extremely injudicious conduct of some of its supporters. The Usher saw fit to make a scurrilous attack on the chairman of the committee in the local press, the pseudonym under which he wrote being no less arrogant a title than " *Rex* Persarum ! " Some of the chairman's more ill-advised friends retaliated by attacking the Usher in a similar strain. Then followed a long anonymous correspondence, full of virulent abuse and mutual recrimination, which did neither side any good and the Perse a vast deal of harm. Both inside and outside the school things soon became intolerable. The climax was reached one memorable day when the Usher and another Master fell out over some trivial dispute, and

" came not only to bitter words, but to actual *blows* in the middle of the school-room, aided and abetted by the shouts and jeers of all the boys. All this sounds incredible and, of course, is quite impossible nowadays : but it actually happened some fifty years ago." [1]

[1] *Pelican*, December, 1909, p. 78.

After this the governors had to intervene, and both the combatants beat an ignominious retreat. The governors decided that it was time that a younger man had charge of the Perse, and so Peter Mason retired. For his past services he was awarded a well-merited pension. He did not live long to enjoy it, dying in 1868. He did good work for the school, when he was in his prime, and gratitude demands that this good work, and none of the evils which befell the Perse in his latter days, should live after him. It was his misfortune that his retirement was rendered necessary owing to circumstances over which ill-health prevented him from having any control.

Towards the end of Mason's Mastership strong representations had been made to the Trustees about the neglect of classical teaching. In 1864 this defect was remedied. A Johnian, like his predecessor, Frederic Heppenstal was more of an all-round man. Not only was he a ninth Classic but also a senior Optime. During the eleven years he was at the Perse the school underwent a complete change. Discipline, which had been so deplorably lax in the late fifties and early sixties, went altogether to pieces during the interregnum which preceded his appointment. Even optimists prophesied that it would take many years to infuse a right spirit

into the school, but such was Heppenstal's per-
sonality that not only did disorder soon become a
thing of the past, but there grew up a healthy
patriotism which has been of lasting benefit to the
school. Although his manner was somewhat
austere, and constant ill health occasionally inclined
him to be irritable, those of his pupils who got
to know him well found he was endowed with
genuine kindheartedness and unbounded liberality.
A strict disciplinarian, he earned the respect and
affection of all his pupils, and indeed of all people
who can admire a good man endeavouring to do his
duty in the face of an incurable disease.

Heppenstal at once set to work to make school
life more real outside as well as inside the classroom.
He threw himself heart and soul into the boys'
games and frequently took part in them himself.
Athletics were by no means a novelty at the Perse.
As early as 1856 cricket had obtained official
recognition, for in September of that year the
governors gave a whole holiday on the occasion of
a match against Lynn School. Even before this
the Perse had produced prominent local players ;
A. J. D. Diver (adm. 1836) was the principal bowler
for Cambridge Town in the days when the
University had no easy task to beat that club,
and C. J. Hutt (adm. 1835) used to play for the

University in the forties.   But games, such as they were, formed no part of the school life until Heppenstal's time.   Until then the cricket and football teams were merely voluntary organisations got up amongst the boys themselves.   Strictly speaking, Heppenstal did not introduce compulsory games, but he made games so popular an institution that it came to be a point of honour with the boys that membership of the school should entail membership of the Games Club.

The reformer's hand was no less active inside the school than out.   Classical teaching made such rapid progress that only two years after Heppenstal's arrival the Endowed Schools Commissioners could report that the results were most encouraging. In time Heppenstal gathered round him a band of earnest students, whom he imbued with his love of classical learning and accuracy.   Many of his boys afterwards figured high in the scholarship lists at Cambridge University.   Five became fellows of their colleges, and of these one, T. J. Lawrence, obtained the unique distinction of being senior in two triposes, Law and Moral Science.   At the same time mathematics were not neglected.   This branch of the school was placed in the charge of Rev. John Wisken, himself an old Persean and a high wrangler.

In providing for instruction in other subjects Heppenstal was severely hampered by the smallness of his staff. At one time a proposal was mooted that paying scholars should be charged special fees, and that these fees should go towards the maintenance of a fourth Master, but the number of paying scholars was so small that nothing came of the plan. In 1866 there were only five non-foundationers, each paying £10 a year in addition to the payments directed by decree of 1841, " and it has been found impossible hitherto to maintain an additional master for so small a number ; but the trustees have resolved that so soon as there should be six paying scholars another master should be engaged." [1] In 1867 a French Master and Drawing Master were engaged. In the same year the two lowest classes were incorporated in an English Department intended for those who were too young to receive or did not require instruction in Greek. In 1868 the advent of a sixth non-foundationer enabled the Trustees to appoint a fourth regular Master. During the next seven years further additions were made to the staff. Before he left, Heppenstal had seven assistants, including a Science Master appointed in 1873.

These later additions to the staff were rendered possible as the result of a general re-arrangement of

[1] Report of Endowed Schools Commission, 1864-8.

the Perse Trust under a scheme sanctioned by Her
Majesty in Council on August 9th, 1873. In
Cambridge there had prevailed for some time past
a feeling that the school ought to be placed under
the control of a body less independent of municipal
influence.[1] The committee appointed by the Town
Council in 1861 was not altogether inactive, and had
agitated for a new constitution for the Perse with a
governing body on which the municipality should
be adequately represented. The injudicious news-
paper warfare, to which reference has already been
made, for a time retarded progress in this direction.
The Inspector of Endowed Schools, who visited the
Perse in 1866, gave the movement very little
encouragement.

"There can be no doubt," he said, "that the existing
body of trustees is well qualified to deal with all educational
questions arising in connection with the school, and being on
the spot, their advice and assistance is readily obtainable.
The establishment of an English department too shows that
they have no wish to make the course of instruction in any
way exclusive or to restrict it to those for whom a high class
or 'liberal' education is desired. Probably the only disadvantage attending the present institution consists in the

[1] The first movement in favour of municipal control dates back
to 1842. In that year it was proposed to convene a meeting to
protest against the refusal of Caius College to award a Perse Scholarship to an old Persean, who had done well in his May examination.
As, however, the conveners discovered that they were mistaken as
to facts, the meeting was never held.

check that may be given to the growth of that feeling of common interest which should bind a town to its principal place of education."

Nevertheless, the disadvantage which the Inspector thus airily passed over, was not wholly to be disregarded and was, in fact, appreciated by the Trustees themselves.

The Endowed Schools Commissioners fully realised the necessity for giving the town a voice in the management of the school when in 1873 they approved of the new scheme drawn up under the Endowed Schools Act of 1869. Although numerous alterations have since been made as to details, the salient features of this scheme still exist. The greatest change was that made in the composition of the governing body. The Master and four senior Fellows of Caius College were replaced by fifteen governors. The connection with Caius was, however, perpetuated by conferring on the College the right to nominate three of the members of the new governing body. Of the remaining governors, three were appointed by the University, six were appointed by the Town Council, and the remainder were co-opted. The co-opted members were appointed for six years and the others for three.

The old titles of Master, Usher, and Assistant

Usher were exchanged for those of Headmaster and Assistant Masters. The Headmaster was in future to be paid partly by a fixed salary and partly by capitation fees. The school was divided into two departments—a junior and a senior. The former was the same as the English Department established in 1866 and subsequently acquired the appellation of the Commercial Side, by which name it was known until Sides were abolished in 1902. The Junior Department was intended for boys between the ages of eight and sixteen, who were required to pay only half the fees payable in the other Department. For the Senior Department Greek was compulsory, and the boys were permitted to remain until they were nineteen. At the same time the number of free places was reduced to twenty-five, but these were still restricted to natives of Cambridge, Barnwell, Chesterton, and Trumpington. The Perse Scholarships and Fellowships at Caius had already come to an end, having been merged in the common scholarship fund of that college by the University Commissioners in 1860. After that date boys from the Perse ceased to have any preference in election to scholarships at Caius, but no compensation was made to the school for this loss.

The greatest change of all effected by the new

scheme was the establishment of a school for girls. This was placed under the charge of ten managers, six being appointed by the governing body of the boys' school and four being co-opted.

At the same time, steps were taken for the partition of the trust property and the assignment of a portion thereof to the new governors for the sole use of the school. The Order in Council directed that land and securities should be handed over to the governors representing roughly two-sevenths of the whole trust income. The scheme for partition was not actually sanctioned until February 3rd, 1880, when the governors received the Manor of Frating (subject to certain rights thereover reserved to the Perse Trustees), two farms comprising about four hundred and fifty acres, and woodlands comprising about one hundred acres in the parish of Frating, and a sum of £6,228 2s. 1d. in Consols. Out of the rents and dividends accruing therefrom an annual sum of £150, or in lieu thereof one quarter of the total income, was to be paid to the managers of the girls' school. The Frating property was held until 1913, when it was sold to provide the purchase money for a site adjoining the boys' school. At the time of the partition it was valued at £20,000, but during the agricultural depression in the last century the property depreciated considerably. For a long time it was found impossible to pay the full contribution to the girls' school.

Heppenstal remained at the Perse for two years after the introduction of the new scheme. In 1875 he left to take up the Headmastership of Sedbergh School, where his work enhanced the reputation he had already won at the Perse. Unhappily a career full of promise was cut short by sudden death.

CHAPTER VIII

THE LAST FIFTY YEARS

THE last fifty years cover approximately the Head-masterships of J. B. Allen (1875-84), H. C. Barnes-Laurence (1884-1902), and W. H. D. Rouse (since 1902). For reasons, which are easily apparent, it is not possible to do adequate justice in the present chapter to all that has happened in the history of the Perse during that period. Never theless, so many important developments, deeply affecting the fortunes of the Perse, have occurred that a history of the school would be incomplete without some mention of them.

One of the greatest changes of all during the period under review was undoubtedly the trans-plantation of the school from Free School Lane to Hills Road. For some years prior to 1888 Cam-bridge University had been buying up the site of what had once been the close of the Augustinian Friars. By the beginning of that year all the land except that occupied by the school and the Perse

Almshouses had been acquired, and negotiations were begun for the purchase of the remaining strip of land. The school premises were too confined for the increased number of boys then attending the Perse, and the University's previous purchases had rendered expansion on the Free School Lane site impossible. Except on grounds of sentiment, no objection could be raised to the acquisition of the site by the University. Caius College offered for sale another site on Hills Road, which the governors purchased for £4500. The old premises were sold for £12,000, and others erected on the new site from the designs of W. M. Fawcett, at a cost of £14,500. In 1890 the new school was ready for the reception of masters and boys, and the migration took place. The buildings were formally opened at a public banquet at which the Rt. Hon. H. C. Raikes (then Postmaster-General) and the late Sir Richard Jebb were the principal speakers. Some of the interesting rooms of the old school were incorporated in the Engineering Laboratory which took its place, and the fine old Jacobean roof was preserved. Externally, however, not a trace of the old school is now left. The Headmaster's house stood until 1912, but was pulled down in that year to make room for an extension of the Laboratory.

To the new school buildings was added in 1892

(with the assistance of a grant from the Cambridge Borough Council) a chemical laboratory. Other additions (including an armoury for the Officers' Training Corps) have been made in more recent years. The site was enlarged in 1914 by the acquisition of the house adjoining it on the south side.

A playing field off Luard Road was acquired in 1906 from Trinity College. Until that date the Games Club had never owned a field, but had had to be content with the very unsatisfactory expedient of sharing Parker's Piece with other clubs. A miniature rifle range was constructed on the playing field entirely by members of the school. When the Perse was removed to Hills Road, neither Headmaster nor Second Master was provided with a house on the new site. For a long time the masters had to find what quarters they could in the town. These premises were generally ill-adapted for the reception of boarders. Want of funds unfortunately prevented the governors from erecting boarding houses, and the matter of accommodation was left in a more or less unsatisfactory state until 1911. In that year the present Headmaster and Mr. I. H. Hersch each built a suitable house on land near to the playing field. The Perse owes a debt of gratitude to both of them, for these buildings were erected at their own expense. The arrival of boarders recalls the former days of the school's prosperity in the seventeenth century. In September 1910 the Preparatory Department was removed from the school buildings to Bateman House, thus releasing two class-rooms urgently needed for the increasing numbers.

Perhaps the most far-reaching change, which has occurred during the period under review, is that which took place in 1902. It will be remembered that in 1866 an English Department was established, which subsequently came to be known as the Commercial Side. From that date until 1900 the Perse was conducted as a dual school with Classical and Commercial Sides. In 1899 there were approximately 210 boys in the school. Of these, some thirty were in the preparatory department, and the remainder roughly divided as to two-thirds in the Commercial and as to one-third on the Classical Side. Boys on the latter side paid a higher fee, and the two sides were kept separate and distinct not only as regards educational work but also to a very considerable degree as regards recreation and general school life. Such an organisation required an unusually large staff, and suffered from many obvious disadvantages. In the autumn of 1900 the Cambridgeshire Education Committee established in

Cambridge a County School for Boys, where courses in technical and commercial subjects could be obtained at a very cheap cost. The Perse was at this time in serious financial straits, and it became apparent that with a competitor in the field the dual organisation must be abandoned. It was therefore decided that the school should be developed as a single school on the lines of the Classical Side, and that provision for the teaching required on the Commercial Side should be left in other hands.

Of the actual work of the school in the earlier part of the period covered by this chapter, little need be said. When Mr. Barnes-Laurence was appointed Headmaster in 1884 there were less than 100 boys : in a few years he not only doubled the numbers, but immensely improved the efficiency of the school in all directions, and raised its tone and the standard of discipline. The record of scholarships and other successes at the Universities bear testimony to the good teaching of the school, while his influence on character, and encouragement of athletics and other sides of school life were no less marked. A keen cricketer himself, he set an example of interest in games, and introduced sound methods of administration and the " conduct of business " which have been of service to his pupils in after-life. The period of his Headmastership saw the establishment or revival of the Annual Athletic Sports (in 1887), of the School Debating Society, and of the school magazine, *The Pelican.*

By a sad coincidence, he passed away within a few weeks of these lines being penned.

The important change in the constitution of the school to which allusion has been made virtually coincided with the appointment as his successor in 1902 of Dr. W. H. D. Rouse, late Fellow of Christ's College.   Perhaps no other Headmaster in the long history of English public school education has been surrounded by so able, so generous, and so devoted a body of workers and colleagues as Dr. Rouse. All in their persons and respective departments have contributed to a scheme of reform which is both comprehensive and unique.   The time has not yet come to make public so intimate a record of unselfish labour and self-sacrifice.   Suffice it to say that in time to come their names will be familiar to all who care to study one of the most remarkable and most successful experiments ever made in the history of English education.   The curriculum of the Perse can now justly claim to be an "all subjects" curriculum.   It has been built up by the united efforts of Dr. Rouse and his staff, working on broad principles which govern not only its plan as a whole but also the methods applied to its special or component parts. The object of the instructors is to unite throughout in a greater or lesser degree both mental and bodily activities. Premature specialisation is avoided, and the pupil's mind is not overloaded with more new work than it can undertake at any one moment. By gradual process the master takes his pupil from what is known and what is concrete or easy to what is difficult, abstract, and unknown, and in the process the boy retains his vivacity and his interest in the acquiring of knowledge.

It was on account of his teaching of Languages, and especially the Classics, that Dr. Rouse first attracted the attention of educationalists to the Perse School. He has applied not only to French and German, but also to Greek and Latin the natural or direct method, wherein experience is associated with expression and the idea with the spoken word. Chiefly owing to the success which has attended the experiments at the Perse this method has in recent years been adopted for the teaching of Modern Languages in other progressive schools. Dr. Rouse has shown that the same method meets with conspicuous success when applied to Classical teaching. After all, as he says, " the Romans used Latin and the Greeks used Greek to express their daily thoughts to one another," and there is no reason why life should not be breathed into what too often in the past has been the dry bones of Classics.

The direct method has produced remarkable results in the teaching of French, in great measure due to the skill and devotion of Mr. L. C. de Glehn. Perhaps the most noticeable thing is the excellence of the pupils' French pronunciation. It is often hard to believe that some of the boys who have learnt French at the Perse have not acquired their accents in France. There have been some very successful productions of French plays, including de Banville's *Gringoire*, performed in 1919.

Experience has shown that the average boy can with little difficulty take four languages during the course of his school career and learn them thoroughly. At the Perse a boy's early years are devoted to a thorough grounding in English. At the age of ten he will begin to learn French by the direct method. Other languages are taken up at intervals of approximately two years. At the age of twelve a boy will have learnt to express himself easily in French, and will begin to study Latin. Two years later Latin will be followed by Greek, and at sixteen he will tackle German. When the fourth language is begun, French is dropped except for occasional reading to keep it fresh. In the teaching of each of these languages special attention is paid to pronunciation, and the speaking of the language precedes the writing of it. When the boy has by speaking learnt also to express himself in writing he turns to composition. He is not surfeited with the endless string of meaningless sentences for translation and set pieces of prose which have driven the love of languages out of so many schoolboys in the past. In Latin composition, for instance, he will in the first instance be told a story in Latin and then be required to paraphrase it from memory. At a further stage he will be given the résumé of a story and be expected to enlarge thereon. Later still he will be given a theme.

Equal care is bestowed throughout the boy's school career on the teaching of English. In this subject the Perse has been fortunate in having the services of Mr. Caldwell Cook, the author of the "Play Way." He has proved what a vast deal can be done to instil into boys a genuine love for all that is highest and best in English literature. Boys are encouraged to write ballads and plays. They also give lectures to their forms on a variety of subjects. After the lecture has been delivered, the criticism of the form is invited and freely given. All these proceedings are taken by the boys as a matter of course, and by this system the boy-lecturer is saved from the tendency to priggishness which might be expected. He retains his natural boyishness, and with the co-operation not only of his Master but also of his schoolfellows learns to put pleasurable pursuits to real and valuable use. With a longing to create he acquires the ability to justify his ambition.

Great scope for giving practical expression to this creative enthusiasm is found in the dramatic performances which are staged by the boys each term. It is the Headmaster's ambition that handicraft, embroidery and kindred crafts should be linked up with literature and other intellectual studies. Thus, when it has been decided to act a certain play, the actors would make the furniture for the stage in their carpenter's shop, would design, cut out, and make their own costumes and embroider them themselves. It is a great idea, and has already in part been carried out.

Outside the class-room the inauguration of numerous societies and institutions has done much to stimulate school life and school patriotism. Boys are thus brought together after lessons, and the corporate feeling is fostered. Among these institutions the Perse Players is one of the most important. Their productions have included plays of Shakespeare and classical drama. The Players have also staged pieces written by members of the society, some of which have been reviewed not unfavourably in the London press, and have appeared in print in the Perse Playbooks. A perusal of the printed plays shows the reader how true and deep a love of all that is best in the English language has been instilled into the boys at the Perse School. In the plays and poems which are to be found in the playbooks there is none of the juvenile precocity which repels the reader as being forced and unnatural, but all the boyish naturalness which has so often in the past been stifled by the process of forcing.

The numbers at the Perse School have increased remarkably during Dr. Rouse's Headmastership : in 1902 there were 139 boys (the numbers having fallen considerably owing to the establishment in 1900 of the County School for Boys, referred to above, pp. 142, 143) ; there are now over 360.

The Perse Union Society is a debating society which can with justification claim to stand in a marked position amongst school debating societies. Visitors' debates are held at frequent intervals, and maintain a high level. The principal officers of the Cambridge University Union Society have regularly accepted invitations to the School Society's meetings, when speakers from amongst the boys have taken leading parts in the debates.

Mention must be made of the School magazine, which has taken its title of *The Pelican* from the

School crest. It is by no means the earliest school magazine. In Mr. Heppenstal's time there came out every year a magazine called the *Perse School Christmas Annual*—subsequently abbreviated to the *Perse School Annual*. It never seems to have obtained official recognition. Fiction filled most of the pages, and the chronicling of school events was not considered to be one of its necessary functions. The earliest number now known to be extant is that of 1874, edited by H. T. O. and A. G. O. Pain under the pseudonym of "The Siamese Twins."[1] In the next year's *Annual* are some verses by the Editor's brother, Barry Pain—the first composition, it is believed, of that writer to appear in print. No terminal magazine was published until the *Pelican* came into being in 1889. This magazine is now well past its majority and leads a flourishing existence.

Sport has not been neglected. The games were re-organised in 1905 and the school divided into houses. Association football gave way to Rugby in 1907, and the Perse is now able to put a powerful fifteen in the field. Hockey was introduced at the same time. As evidence that this branch of school life has received attention, it may be mentioned that in inter-university contests old

[1] See illustration, facing p. 66.

Perseans have figured in the cricket, athletic, association football and hockey teams of the rival universities.

Another branch of school activity, a cadet corps, was established soon after the close of the Second Boer War, and obtained official recognition in 1905. Under Lord Haldane's scheme it was converted into an Officers' Training Corps, and, as such, prior to the recent war gained a higher percentage of certificates of efficiency than any other school in the country. The valuable work done in this branch of school life soon came to be realised. During the European War several hundreds of its past members gained commissions and served with distinction.

Undoubtedly the most important and most valuable of all the school institutions which have sprung up during the last twenty-five years has been the Old Persean Society. It was founded at a meeting which was held in the school in December, 1901. Ever since that date its members have followed the fortunes of the school with close interest, and, whenever it lay in their power, have given evidence of their loyalty by practical support. In 1906 the Society came boldly into the field to champion the cause of the Perse. The financial condition of the school was at the time very critical indeed. The Society convened a public meeting on July 11th of that year for the purpose of enlisting outside support. Amongst the speakers who urged the claims and needs of the school upon public attention were Lord Lytton, Sir George Fordham, Sir Walter Durnford, and the late Professor S. H. Butcher. A subscription list was opened immediately, and amongst the subscribers were Mr. Arthur Balfour and the late Duke of Devonshire. The sum of money then raised not only provided a reserve at a grave financial crisis, but also helped towards the purchase of the school playing ground. At a later date financial assistance was also offered towards the building of the boarding houses. In 1914 the Society undertook the raising of a Tercentenary Fund for the furthering of the many necessary projects which must be set on foot if the school is to prosper in the future. Just before this a movement with similar objects had been started by friends of the school, and the two schemes were combined, but owing to the war action was suspended for some time. By 1919 a considerable sum had been raised, under the title of the Tercentenary and War Memorial Fund, which in that year provided the means for buying Gonville House, standing next the school on the North. The purchase, towards which

Caius College contributed £250, has added greatly to the size and to the value of the present school site.

Negotiations are now in progress for the acquisition of additional land, greatly needed for games, adjoining the present playing-field. It is hoped that the Fund will in time be sufficiently augmented not only to provide for this, but also to enable a new school to be erected on this site capable of meeting the growing needs of the school, and in every way worthy of the place which it holds in education, for which the present buildings are quite inadequate. The Governors have decided on this policy, but are unable to carry it out until financial conditions permit.

In November 1919 the Old Persean Society held a Tercentenary Dinner in the School Hall. The number of distinguished guests made the occasion memorable. Their Royal Highnesses, the Prince Albert and Prince Henry, then in residence at the University, were present, the former replying to the toast of " The Royal Family." The Marquis of Crewe proposed the toast of " The School," and the Bishop of Woolwich, an Old Persean, was in the chair.

Mr. H. P. Cooke, who has been a secretary of the Society since its foundation, has spared neither time nor energy in directing its various activities, and particularly in organising the Tercentenary Fund. During the same period the post of treasurer has been conscientiously filled by Mr. Roger Smart ; Mr. P. J. Spalding for several years did invaluable work as secretary, while, as chairman of the Executive Committee and of the Tercentenary and War Memorial Committee, Mr. E. Saville Peck has rendered devoted service.

Benefactions and financial assistance have also been forthcoming in the past from other sources. Trinity College has of recent years given the school generous support. In 1884, when certain alms-houses attached to the College were closed, the endowments were diverted to the foundation of scholarships at the Perse. In 1909 the same College also established three leaving exhibitions tenable at the University. The Cambridge Town and County Councils both make generous grants in aid of the school. The County Council is now granting £1200 annually ; the Town Council, though the Borough contributes its proportional share of this £1200, gives £400 in addition. The Board of Education has bestowed on the Perse (which shares that distinction with four other secondary schools) a special annual grant " so that the experimental work there being done in the teaching of Classics

can be carried out more thoroughly." Acknowledg-
ment must also be made of the valuable help given
in many forms by Lady Frazer, whose advice and
assistance have always been at the disposal of the
Modern Language department.

Mention may be made of the last four Chairmen
of the Governors. Mr. J. Hamblin Smith, of
Gonville and Caius College, was chairman from
1897 to 1901. He had a very intimate knowledge
of the history of the school and was known not only
to the Governors, but, by his frequent and welcome
visits, to the masters and boys. The Rev. J. B.
Lock, Bursar of Caius College, was chairman from
1901 to 1904, a period covering the critical days
already mentioned when it was decided to abolish
the Commercial Side. Mr. A. I. Tillyard of St.
John's College showed an active devotion to the
school's interests during his long term of the chairmanship (1904-1920). Particular attention may be
called to the way in which he brought the financial
needs of the school to the notice of the various
public bodies that now help it, and of his activities
in negotiating the purchase of the playing-field.
The school may have every confidence that it will
be well served by Mr. G. Brimley Bowes of Emmanuel College, who, as an old boy, an active
member of the Old Persean Society, and for the

last few years a devoted member of the Board of Governors, is admirably suited to holding the chairmanship to which he has recently been elected.

A school's prosperity and usefulness is often judged by the numbers and successes of its pupils, and the Perse could well afford to be judged by these standards. But Perseans would fain have their school judged not by its scholarship successes and honours list, but by the measure in which it has contributed to the good of the State. The European War has given the opportunity of putting the school to this test. Not only were refugees from Belgium and Serbia received in the school during their exile from their own country, but in the field Perseans of all generations played an honourable part. During the war, as far as can be ascertained from available records, over 530 " old boys " were on military service, and the decorations won include seven D.S.O.'s, one D.S.C., four M.C.'s and Bar, twenty-nine M.C.'s, seventeen of the various grades of the Order of the British Empire, and a number of other British and Foreign decorations. Of the number who served eighty-six did not return, and in their honour a Memorial Tablet[1] is placed in the School Hall: it was unveiled on 21st May, 1921, by General Lord Horne, G.O.C. in Chief, Eastern

[1] Provided from the Fund described above, p. 152.

THE SCHOOL WAR MEMORIAL

Command. The design was a labour of love on the part of an Old Persean, Mr. Cyrus Johnson. The Roll of the Fallen is too grievously long for mention to be here made of every Persean who has made the great sacrifice, but it is a proud record of the spirit which has pervaded the school through many generations. The greatness to which the Perse has attained has been purchased by those who were " not wanting to the city with their virtue, but made unto it an honourable contribution." The memory of this sacrifice will inspire in those who remain and those who follow after a sure hope that their school will rise to even further greatness in the years to come.

INDEX

GLASGOW: PRINTED AT THE UNIVERSITY PRESS BY ROBERT MACLEHOSE AND CO. LTD.